QUALITY:
WHAT MAKES IT HAPPEN?

■

Norman B. Reilly

VAN NOSTRAND REINHOLD
New York

Library of Congress Catalog Card Number 93-13457
ISBN 0-442-01635-2

I(T)P Van Nostrand Reinhold is an International Thomson Publishing Company.
       ITP logo is a trademark under license.

Printed in the United States of America.

Van Nostrand Reinhold   International Thomson Publishing GmbH
115 Fifth Avenue   Königswinterer Str. 518
New York, New York 10003   5300 Bonn 3
                                   Germany
International Thomson Publishing
Berkshire House, 168-173   International Thomson Publishing Asia
High Holborn   38 Kim Tian Rd., #0105
London WC1V7AA   Kim Tian Plaza
England   Singapore

Thomas Nelson Australia   International Thomson Publishing Japan
102 Dodds Street   Kyowa Building, 3F
South Melbourne 3205   2-2-1 Hirakawacho
Victoria, Australia   Chiyada-Ku, Tokyo 102
                                   Japan
Nelson Canada
1120 Birchmount Road
Scarborough, Ontario
M1K 5G4, Canada

16 15 14 13 12 11 10 9 8 7 6 5 4 3 2 1

Library of Congress Cataloging-in-Publication Data

Reilly, Norman B.
    Quality : what makes it happen? / Norman B. Reilly.
    p.   cm.
    Includes bibliographical references (p.   ) and index.
    ISBN 0-442-01635-2
    1. Total quality management—Handbooks, manuals, etc.   I. Title.
    HD62.15.R44   1994
    658.5'62—dc20
                                                     93-13457
                                                         CIP

To Patricia Marion Donnelly—Talk About Quality

CONTENTS

INTRODUCTION

■ When once asked to review a volu-
minous manuscript, Winston Churchill is said to have re-
marked, "The length of this document defends it well against
the risk of it being read."

This book is short for a reason. An increasing number of *busy*
people throughout government and industry are being exposed
to Total Quality Management (TQM) and are asking, "What
is it?" and "How will it affect me?" If you are among that
number, this book will provide, in a single sitting, a valuable
and concise introduction into the world of modern quality.

When finished, you will hopefully find additional time to
pursue the subject. If survival in the United States is part of
your scheme, you will definitely find time. This offering is
designed to increase the probability of that happening. It all has
to do with the expansion of the word "quality" and the
acceptance of its newer meaning over the past half century in
Japan and in the United States.

The traditional concept of quality control in the United States is quite different from the more successful Japanese version of quality. In the United States, quality control has historically been based largely on improving quality through *testing*. The philosophy inherently accepts that there is a tolerable level of failure in production or in the delivery of services. The concept identifies quality control as a downstream measuring function that monitors. It comes after the fact.

In Japan, quality is built in upstream through the involvement of *suppliers* to an organization, the combined roles of *management* and *workers* within the organization, an understanding of complete *system-wide process*, downstream identification of *customer* preferences, and a revolutionary *change* in the way managers think and behave.

The roots of these ideas lie in a number of important writings that have appeared over the last 50 years, dealing with the organization of work at both the managerial and worker levels that are directly related to the nurturing of motivation, innovation, pride, and quality. These invaluable efforts, summarized in Part 1, have been advanced by psychiatrists, psychologists, sociologists, educators, and perceptive professional managers.

Unquestionably, the most noted work devoted to the matter of quality has been that of one W. Edwards Deming. This is due not only to the ideas that Deming has synthesized, but to his dramatic ability to influence their successful implementation across government, production, and service industries.

While Deming holds a B.S. degree in physics from the University of Wyoming (1921), an M.S. degree in mathematics and physics from the University of Colorado (1924), and a Ph.D. in mathematical physics from Yale University (1928), he is far from what we look upon as an academic. Those who know him would likely find that comment amusing. The fact is that Deming does not waste much time indulging in niceties in the spreading of his message, and he spreads it like an attacking dynamo. His modus operandi is one of irreverent shock—a quick and effective method of determining the open-mindedness of the recipient of his feisty onslaughts. He has routinely been perceived by managers in the United States as a pompous egomaniac. On these occasions, he simply goes someplace else—plenty of others are waiting for him.

Quality has emerged differently in Japan, where managers typically focus on any and all concepts that even hint of the possibility of product or service improvement. The Japanese manager is simply problem oriented, not personality oriented. If you suggest to Japanese managers that there may be a better way of doing business, they will listen to your idea with enthusiasm. If you turn out to be right, you will have made life-long friends. While the Japanese workplace is highly aggressive, the element of fear, as it is experienced in the United States, is not one of its driving motivations.

How did Japan get that way? Historical reasons are given in Part 1. Deming has a shorter answer. He is fond of stating that he *did not export American practice*. Deming succinctly presents his thesis in his Fourteen Points for quality improvement. These are covered in Part 2.

Part 3, "The New Quality in Action," provides examples of attempts to implement the new revolution in our country—some good, some not so good. Not all the material is complimentary. The treatment is not intended to be pedantic nor contemptuous, but to assist in raising levels of our own awareness. Part 4 offers top-level generic guidelines for implementing a modern quality program.

First, a quick setting for the coming trauma.

Here are some typical Deming viewpoints on management, process within an organization, the workers, and fear in the workplace. If you are a manager in the United States, you

probably won't agree with the following Demingistic synopsis, at least not at the outset.
Sit down someplace. Hold on.

- Management—The problem with our competitiveness on the world stage in both goods and services is related to high labor rates, production costs, union demands, government policies, tariffs, deficits, and politics. These and other factors have strapped our managers—the best in the world. In the United States, managers have achieved their status through experience and a proven ability to utilize that experience effectively. If they didn't, how could they be there?
Wrong!
The problem *is* management. In the United States, managers typically achieve their status through a set of circumstances totally unrelated to their ability to do anything. Because they are schooled to lead by "taking personal charge" and believe themselves to be knowledgeable, they tend to concoct organizational strategies based on their own fields of limited expertise, without sufficient benefit of the insights of workers, middle management, suppliers, or customers.
CEOs with financial backgrounds invariably lead differently than CEOs with production backgrounds. Taking the lead from those who work for you is a weakness in the United States. In Japan it is a strength. Good managers formulate their strategies by listening to *everybody* and by recognizing what they don't know. Unilateral concoction of narrow policies, such as those fostered through Management by Objective, are destructive because they focus on short-term goals and can only be achieved at the expense of other factors. Goals such as "increasing market share," "reducing production costs," "increasing revenues," and so on can all be achieved in isolation at the expense of quality. It is long-term quality that brings everything else to an organization—and quality should be defined by the

customers' needs and perceptions, not by engineers and managers.

- Process—A basic tenet in the United States is that quality is enhanced by concentration on the integrity of the product. Wrong! Quality is the natural fallout of a never-ending examination of an entire system process, involving suppliers, everyone in the accomplishing organization, and customers. Quality is achieved by identifying the nature of variance in process and by forever striving to reduce that variance—not by simple inspection, meeting specifications, or "delivering" a service.

- Workers—Workers are most productive when each is given a specific, well-defined task, is trained to do it, is reviewed, rated, and corrected when necessary, and is compensated through ranking. Wrong! The reason that workers cannot do any better than they are is because they are constrained physically and emotionally by processes and configurations and by the fear established by management. It is the existing system in which the worker is embedded that controls innovation and productivity. Not the worker. Banging on the workers can't change an inefficient system. Nor can the workers change the existing system—but managers can. The way to increase innovation, productivity, and quality is to empower workers and middle managers by letting them out of their cartons and giving them more team responsibility with which to perform their jobs.

- Fear—Slogans and motivators, such as zero defects, quotas, incentives, and annual reviews, are valuable tools for maintaining and increasing innovation and productivity. Wrong!

Such competitive tactics drive workers against each other and reward them for finding or inventing ways to pad figures and generally fool the "system." These tactics basically produce an atmosphere of fear. There is a great deal of fear in the United States working environment, including government at all levels. Not only does such fear promote the wrong kind of competition between workers, it also creates a reluctance to convey information horizontally and vertically, up and down the management chain. Information hiding is prolific in the United States, both within our organizations and in our affiliations with customers and vendors. Bad news is routinely hidden because organizations and the people in them are simply afraid. In Japan, bad news is good news because the culture is oriented toward fixing things—not hiding them.

That's only the beginning. Deming himself would have been far less civilized. But if the man is anywhere close to pointing the way—and there is a lot of evidence to aver that he is—more of us need to fess up and get primed for an immense transformation. I mean large!

PART 1

THE ORIGINS AND MATURATION OF MODERN QUALITY

■ Something else happened in 1776. On March 8 of that year, James Watt, at age 40, turned on the first steam engine that actually worked. The machine was used for pumping water out of a mine. A crowd of overjoyed onlookers yelped wildly as the blustering contrivance spewed black liquid across the plain—a cheer soon to be heard round the world.

"Mr. Watt," said Matthew Boulton, owner of half-interest in the marvel before them, "I hope and flatter myself that we are at the eve of a fortune" (Browne 1942, 2). They were.

What happened that day not far from Birmingham, England, would lift incredibly and forever our total reliance on the muscles of humans and beasts. The machine would change every institution and activity known to humanity. What we preached and believed, our economics, cities and countrysides, laws, politics, education, science, medicine, engineering, arts, wars, class structures, and environment, our concepts of progress, and our very dreams—virtually every aspect of human life—was to change drastically and with unprecedented speed. As a result of that day, following ages of sweat, unfathomable toil, and want, we have soared in a mere two centuries to a proliferation of goods to the masses—reapers, sowers, gins, fabrics, plastics, cars, ships, trains, planes, and rockets to the stars.

Mr. Watt's machine also created a setting for significant changes in the way we think about and accept quality—a reformation whose sophistication has exponentially grown its own wings in the latter half of the twentieth century.

In the early nineteenth century, quality was not among the foremost of issues—not when just a century earlier one person in five hundred wore stockings and suddenly not one in a thousand was without them. Any stocking was better than none. The aristocrats, of course, still donned their handmade hose of the highest quality. As the elite saw it, production goods were suitable for the masses, but did not carry the quality status of goods produced by traditional craftsmen. But for humbler classes, reaping the benefits of production—the relatively sudden availability of blankets, pants, shirts, shoes, cooking utensils, tools, and a myriad of other products so useful in daily life—must have spurred a demand so high that the mere act of acquisition likely eclipsed any issues of marginal quality.

Demand would continue until its decline prompted an age of imperialism designed to open and control still new markets. The "good" emerging industrial savages took from the "bad" savages. The basic economic tenet of the nineteenth and early twentieth centuries was clear and simple. Secure larger markets and then do three things—produce, produce, produce.

If quality was an issue throughout this period, it is not well documented. What is well known is that the workers had other things to think about—among them, the intolerable conditions of labor that the rising capitalist wave imposed. The new capitalist elite raised exploitation to a structured art. Fear and economic bondage in the form of widespread indebtedness to employers, 12-hour days, 6-day weeks, child labor excesses, and insufferable working and living conditions were regarded by these new capitalists as essential to driving the new economic system. While most of these abuses are less common today, it is interesting to note that basic attitudes and practices of that culture are still steadfastly ingrained in the way that many presently organize and do business. Still with us today is the traditional industrial engineering practice of dividing work into small components and assigning individual workers, or organizational departments, to restricted, specialized tasks.

The concept was given formal credibility through the publication of *Principles of Scientific Management* by Frederick W. Taylor in 1911. Taylor espoused the reduction of each job into its most divisible parts along with their assignments to individual workers. This was done in the name of efficiency. The divide-and-assign paradigm stood Henry Ford well throughout the 1920s, when mass production became the way to do business. Taylor and the United States loved it.

Deming has a great deal to say about this strategy. So have others.

In 1963, Eric Trist and his research colleagues referred to this management approach as "conventional" (Trist et al. 1963). Their work included studies of the application of the conventional management approach to the British mining industry. Work was divided into detailed functions that were assigned to individuals. Quality control was among these separate functions. The conventional paradigm, in theory, is a convenience for management, since the supervision of workers is reduced to simply monitoring intelligent animals engaged in simple, repetitive tasks.

4

What makes the Trist work so important is that the researchers also studied a second organizational structure employed in neighboring British mines—the so-called "composite" structure. In the composite arrangement, teams of miners were formed who were responsible for the total task of coal extraction. Significantly, membership in the teams was determined by the miners themselves, much as a group might choose up teams for a sandlot ball game. The teams managed themselves in a given workplace, including the distribution of wages among themselves. The team was also responsible for their own quality control.

Trist reports remarkable differences in productivity, attitude, and quality between the two concepts of worker organization. The composite work group was highly organized and stable. It was no longer unrealistic for individuals to attain stations of increased importance within the group. The concept of being asked to perform more than a simple task was no longer regarded as exploitation. The opportunity to learn additional skills was actively sought. Supervisors of the groups migrated from issuing orders to simply providing technical advice. They became "leaders" instead of "bosses." They became good guys.

Teams identified problems and were motivated to analyze them and work out ways to fix them. Change was accepted willingly. Attitudes in the workplace transformed dramatically. Absenteeism declined by a whopping 60 percent. An overall improvement of 20 percent was reported, as well as an incredible 42-percent increase in productivity. The groups had social meaning and clear goals.

Because they were empowered in the workplace, *animals became men.*

The inner dynamics of these working groups were not influenced directly by management. This is a significant point. The control of the groups was internal, not external. The idea of simply communicating to workers what their global responsibilities are and then cutting them loose to organize in any manner they wish in order to meet well-defined goals is a very scary one in conventional management. It requires extraordinary change in traditional management lore. Yet the benefits accrued were due to exactly that—management's clear willingness to distribute central power to local structures.

The Trist research group next sought to test the validity of their discoveries in the mines. A similar study was conducted by implementing composite work groups at the Ahmadabad textile mills in Ahmadabad, India. The culture was entirely different. The work force was also different in that it was made up of females. The results were quite similar to those observed previously. Improvements in quality of 30 percent were especially significant.

In 1963, similar results were reported as a result of the implementation of composite work groups at Non-Linear Systems, Inc., a U.S. West Coast manufacturer of electronic test equipment (Kuriloff 1963, 8–17). Again, control of organization, production, test, and quality was taken over by teams. Over a 2-year period, productivity was reported to increase by 30 percent, with a decrease in customer complaints of 7 percent. Improvement continued constantly over time as the groups were persistently self-motivated to identify problems and devise better methods of operation. Quality improved continually, to the near elimination of defects. The role of inspection in quality management diminished greatly.

These examples provide a powerful basis for the counseling of more current observers of the U.S. work scene. While the terms "conventional" and "composite" are not widely used today, several erroneous conventional assumptions remain, under which the majority of our organizations still operate. Traditional management continues to believe:

- Work is detested by everyone.

- Workers have to be cajoled and threatened with penalty in order to achieve organizational objectives.

- They are lazy, dislike challenge, lack ambition, and simply want to be told what to do.

Wrong! The more valid assumptions are:

- Work is a natural enterprise for all of us.

- Workers, when committed to common objectives, will behave more efficiently than management can decree.

- Their commitment will be proportional to the securing of self-esteem and self-development—an opportunity for pride.

Though seemingly slow to catch hold in the United States, the Japanese have widely embraced the concept that management's main function is to eliminate barriers to peoples' enjoyment of work by effectively encouraging everyone to develop themselves through the distribution of both authority and responsibility. The Japanese have embraced the concept that every worker has a right to "joy" in their work.

The new quality is changing concepts of success. Historically, success has been measured by the power and wealth of institutions. Quality demands that success be measured by the pride and self-worth of individuals—a revolutionary idea in Western culture.

One measure of the significance of an idea is its tendency to simultaneously appear, even if the names are different.

Toyota and Bridgestone, both of whom won the coveted Deming Prize in the 1960s, embraced this philosophy through their invention of "policy deployment." The basic principles behind policy deployment are:

1. Top management's total commitment to quality by listening to those people who actually do the work.

2. Middle management's ability to coordinate goal-oriented teams across organizational boundaries, vertically and horizontally.

3. Allowing freedom for the workers and everyone else in the organization to identify problems and come up with innovative solutions through the policy deployment teams. To do this, an organization must eliminate the fear that individuals have associated with bucking the system or of simply being wrong.

The rose has still another name. The breaking down of barriers between departments has also been a major goal of the concept of "Quality Control circles." The QC circle simply consists of representation of workers, supervisors, engineers, and middle management across organizational boundaries to better understand a total process as it affects the improvement of quality. The success of the QC circle approach in Japan has been directly attributable to the intimate support and participation of all levels of management, including top management. This has not been the case in our own country, where attempts at quality improvements have too often been delegated. Typically, QC circles have been installed with a "take-care-of-this" attitude, accompanied by inadequate planning and simplistic expectations of immediate success. When top management did get involved, QC circle membership was often restricted to other top managers. Why? The concept that the lowliest of workers could know more about solving specific problems than their leaders is simply not within the perspective of most American managers. They have been trained to survive in an environment that demands continual self-justification—an adversarial environment where "being right" includes knowing everything, including where and when to dole out credit and blame. To the conventional American manager, listening to workers is akin to admitting a weakness, and weakness is something to fear.

Significantly, for our governments and our service organizations as well, the benefits of top management's commitment to the productive empowerment of workers also apply to the service industries. In 1984, Kansai Electric, a Japanese utility firm, won the Deming Prize. In 1985, Florida Power and Light took a great interest in the successful application by Kansai of TQM in the service industry arena. The top management at FP&L saw policy deployment as an alternative to issuing simple directives through Management by Objective. It was recognized that policy deployment was a crucial ingredient for the institutional acceptance of quality management as it is practiced in Japan.

FP&L went on to build an efficient and more direct feedback mechanism throughout the organization and implemented means of engaging middle management and frontline workers in identifying goals and in constructively involving all personnel toward their attainment. (While this might sound like motherhood, they actually did it!)

Specific target areas for improvement were the reduction of plant shutdowns through false alarms, meter reading errors, and individual customer outages. The workers, many of whom had executed their routine jobs for years, immediately came up with constructive and innovative ideas, for which they had never before been asked. The resulting dramatic improvement through the commitment and motivation of the entire organization resulted in FP&L becoming the first U.S. company to win the Deming Prize.

By any name (composite organization, policy deployment, quality control circles), the direct benefits to quality through implementing these concepts are clearly documented. At least two instructive messages are evident regarding TQM, for those of us who wish to see:

1. Top management cannot implement quality by simply delegating the job to a TQM tsar. U.S. organizations, including the 19 federal agencies targeted by the Office of Management and Budget (OMB), are too filled with *competing* prima donnas who don't want to yield their turf to yet another peer appointee. The intimate and continuous involvement of top management must be ever present.

2. In any organization, the people who are actually doing the work are in the best position to identify and solve problems. The conventional organization excludes workers from these activities. Workers need only be empowered with the unrestricted authority and responsibility to contribute to well-defined goals to reach fuller and more creative potentials. This empowerment is achieved by eliminating hierarchical fear and organizational barriers and meting out responsibility, involvement, and trust. Quality is a direct and dramatic benefactor of these conditions, which can positively motivate workers and managers through their attainment of self-worth, no matter what the job.

The basic tenet of management-inspired team involvement is not the only ingredient required by the modern quality movement. There are other fundamental aspects that have resulted in the maturity of the movement since the 1940s. These include the application of practical tools for understanding and controlling process variation within an organization, as well as the extension of involvement in quality management—

both upstream to suppliers and downstream to consumers—of an organization's goods and services. As a result, the traditional, inwardly directed control concepts of Product Assurance and Quality Assurance have been altered drastically. Logically, the quality movement has also expanded to include considerations of cooperative upstream and downstream movements of quality management.

While the name of Deming is most often associated with the development of modern quality, he has not been the only participant. Other significant players in this maturation have been gentlemen named Homer M. Sarasohn, Walter A. Shewhart, Joseph M. Juran, Armand V. Feigenbaum, and Kaoru Ishikawa, and, of course, a host of associates that made things happen.

But it didn't start here. It started over there.

OVER THERE

At the close of World War II, two significant conditions existed that would determine the course of quality movements in Japan and the United States for the next three decades. The first was the vision that Japan should be guided toward a productive democracy rather than simply punished. The second was that the postwar demand for goods in the United States and throughout the world was immense—a sort of mini-replay of the early nineteenth century call for quantity, quantity, and more quantity.

Early in 1946, a young engineer named Homer Sarasohn arrived in Japan at the request of General Douglas MacArthur. The General wanted reliable radios so that the new order could be heard in every town and village. Sarasohn's charter was to blanket Japan with good radios. In the process of achieving this, he also set in motion a significant sequence of events.

The not yet 30 year old was full of common sense. To Sarasohn, a factory was not a lone entity in itself, but part of a total "system." The system involved materials coming in, the factory itself, other factories, and the means of getting outputs to customers that made them happy.

He was also a firm believer in Statistical Process Control (SPC). SPC is a method of measuring variance in production systems that was developed by Walter Shewhart at Bell Telephone Laboratories some 20 years earlier. So strongly did Sarasohn believe in SPC that he was reluctant at first to provide the Japanese with such a powerful tool. He did, however, use his talent to do more than just build radios. He provided management seminars and instilled concepts of purpose in business beyond that of simply making money. Along the way, he wrote a book entitled *The Industrial Application of Statistical Quality Control.*

Sarasohn sought the direct assistance of Shewhart in the training of Japanese managers, but Shewhart was unavailable. Instead, a student and associate of Shewhart's during the 1930s was invited. The associate's name was W. E. Deming.

In 1950, Deming taught a course to Japanese workers on Elementary Principles of the Statistical Control of Quality. Between 1950 and 1960, 20,000 people were trained in Japan in statistical practices. Despite the fact that students were literally captured and attendance was required, they were avid learners. Deming likes people who want to learn. Deming's view of the worker, executive or otherwise, is that he or she is never too old or too successful to listen and learn.

He had considerable empathy for the plight of his charges, exhibiting both generosity and humility (qualities not often associated with him in the United States). Early in his first visit, Deming also met with the emerging leaders of Japanese industries and professed to them about quality. They listened intently and asked to see him again.

Deming also worked on the national census, applying statistical techniques he developed for the United States Census Bureau during the late 1930s and 1940s. He traveled extensively. Japanese leaders were sufficiently impressed with their rebounding communications industry that they formed the Japanese Union of Scientists and Engineers (JUSE), which was to create the coveted Deming Prize. The prize has been awarded every year since 1951. JUSE remains the focal point of the Japanese quality movement today.

Deming has received his own trophy case of awards, among them a medal from the Emperor of Japan. Significantly, he received a medal from our own President some 28 years later. While we have been slow to listen, Deming's impact on Japan has been phenomenal. Among the long list of examples, in 1980 Japan produced 11 million automobiles, surpassing Detroit for the first time.

When Deming was first teaching in Japan in 1950, Armand Feigenbaum, then manager of quality control at General Electric, published a book called *Total Quality Control* and with it the term TQC was born. Feigenbaum promoted the concept that the pursuit of quality required the coordinated effort of all departments in an organization. He came to this important realization after observing that applications of statistical process control and personnel training efforts in one department still met with opposition and bickering from other departments. The Japanese embraced this idea, but with their own vitally important twist. Feigenbaum's approach was to create a special corps of quality experts to oversee quality at all levels. Due largely to Kaoru Ishikawa, the Japanese concept was to involve *everybody* in the organization with the *direct* responsibility for quality in their own work.

But Feigenbaum did correctly attack the conventional national lore that quality and cost were somehow competing entities. He was among the first to profess that the true achievement of quality actually results in the reduction of costs and that quality was a measurable entity. While his ideas first met with stoic resistance, there is little question among quality experts today that he was dead right.

Joseph M. Juran first got into quality as an employee at Western Electric in the 1920s and later came to know Shewhart. He became a significant contributor to the Japanese movement shortly after his *Quality Control Handbook* was published in 1951. Juran also contributed to the concept that all functions of an organization must be involved in the pursuit of quality. He affirms that the three most vital ingredients of any quality movement are that top management must take an active part, extensive training of all involved parties must take place, and quality improvements must occur at a rapid pace.

The latter, we know, is not always easy. Successful quality movements can typically take 3 to 5 years of hard and diligent work before results flourish. One thing can be said of every successful quality program: They have taken extreme patience, diligent work, and constancy of faith.

Juran understands that good quality programs are not always easy to effect. But he still contends that success can be achieved without the total cultural transformation that Deming insists must take place. Juran finds similarities in the quality movement to other aspects of successful management experience. Deming, on the other hand, asserts that it would be an error to export American management know-how to a friendly nation.

There are other minor differences among the gurus. Juran defines quality as "fit for customer use." Feigenbaum defines quality as "what the customer says it is." Deming differs somewhat. His position is that customers can't always define quality because they don't know how good a provider can be. His example: Customers didn't ask for electric light bulbs before there were any. Still, there is a common thread. Quality is very much customer oriented, and anticipating customer needs is an integral part of staying the quality course.

Kaoru Ishikawa is among the most celebrated of Japanese masters of quality. He was born into a prominent family with a keen awareness of the postwar introduction of quality in Japan. His father, Ichiro Ishikawa, was the gentleman who invited Deming to make presentations to Japanese executives in the early 1950s. The younger Ishikawa began QC circles in 1962 and had sufficient influence to persuade managers to take heed of workers' suggestions. QC circles introduced in the United States in the early 1980s largely lacked that single ingredient. Management put the circles in, but they didn't *listen to what came out*.

Ishikawa was strongly influenced by Deming and Juran. He embraced the concepts of statistical process control, total involvement of all employees (including top management), and an avid orientation toward customer satisfaction and service. He died in 1989, but, through his strong influence and successful dedication, has left a tangible mark on the Japanese quality movement.

OVER HERE

While postwar Japan was busy listening to the new quality gurus, the United States was busy reacting to a product-hungry world. Like our not-too-distant friends of the early nineteenth century, we suddenly had stockings. In this demand environment, almost any management style worked just fine. Long-term vision was not a priority of management nor of stockholders. The boom was on!

Not until the late 1970s and early 1980s did managers in the United States begin to sense a momentum in the East. The story was that it had "something to do with quality." Even then the message was oversimplified. The quality movement in the United States was a virtual disaster between 1980 and 1985, primarily because management's response to the new buzz words was to delegate implementation of partial tools and noncomprehensive solutions. We were stirring, but we didn't get it.

There were also other things going on. The 1980s became the decade of the leveraged buy out, the dismantling of the middle class, and the dehumanization of workers. Attention was focussed on matters other than quality. With deregulation, big business went on a buying spree. Raising money was easy: Simply buy another company, leverage it, and begin to close it down. The future was now. The hyenas were loose. Solid companies were forced to borrow money to raise their stock values in an effort to fight off corporate raiders. During the 1980s, the average number of bankruptcy filings per year in the United States was up more than 150 percent compared to the 1970s and just over 300 percent compared to the 1960s. Combined assets of corporations in bankruptcy reached over $70 billion. Inevitably, no matter what the cause, debt forced plant closures. Hundreds of thousands were cast to the winds as the trickle down trickled down.

Statistics are distant and wintry. The plight of individuals can often have more impact. In their biting book, *America, What Went Wrong?*, Barlett and Steele recount the misfortune of a worker returning from lunch one day. A supervisors meeting was promptly called, and the worker was told that the plant was closing due to restructuring. The issue had nothing to do with quality, just with raising money quickly. There would be no jobs left. That was that. None of the workers had any warning whatsoever (Barlett and Steele 1992, 29).

Still, somehow from 1985 onward quality awareness in the United States began to bud. Now it is actually blossoming. One of the positive factors contributing to this awareness was the establishment of the Malcolm Baldrige National Quality Award, administered by the National Institute of Standards and Technology. An integral and positive purpose of the program is to transfer successful strategies from company to company. In 1991, more than 235,000 applications for the Baldrige Award criteria were requested by U.S. companies, up from 180,000 in 1990, 65,000, in 1989 and 12,000 in 1988 *(Star Free Press,* a 1992).

The federal government and an increasing number of local governments are venturing in as well. In 1987, the Department of Defense, under then-Secretary Frank Carlucci, began implementation of a TQM program. The concept included modifications to the federal acquisition regulations designed to promote quality improvements by involving suppliers in earlier stages of development, closing the gap between research and development, and instituting monetary benefits for both employees and vendors for finding ways to save money. The Secretary had a good idea, but his boss never said very much about it.

A more recent significant federal effort has been launched by the Office of Management and Budget (OMB). The OMB version calls for implementation of TQM in every federal agency through the making of continuous incremental improvements of quality, timeliness, efficiency, and effectiveness of products and services. It won't be easy. Perhaps the ripest area for the application of TQM principles exists within the military materials acquisition process. While reform efforts are underway, contractors still need to deal with alpine piles of gobbledegook requirements. But at least they're "talking the talk" if still learning to "walk the walk." Reports *Aviation Week and Space Technology* (Scott 1990, 75):

> Industry executives and government leaders, however, share the hope that a broad-based shift to TQM principles on both

sides of the procurement process offers the most hope for an improved acquisition environment in the 1990's. TQM's tenets of a two-way customer-serving organization, cultivation of a supplier and subcontract network, and a partnership between industry and government users are being instituted now.

These attitudes, accompanied by a number of successes, are also filtering into other applications throughout the Army, Air Force, and Navy. Says J. Daniel Howard, Under Secretary of the Navy (Howard 1993):

> The Deming principles of process improvement work. We have reduced the F-14 overhaul time by 14 percent and improved our aviation supply office by 44 percent. Now we are moving beyond process control to education, self development, investment in science and technology and sub-optimization through integration. We will have 11,000 people in our school system this year. It works.

The move by OMB and, particularly, its implementation in segments of the Defense Department, has caused a flurry of interest across the aerospace industry. Some experiences have been good and some not so good. Douglas Aircraft went a bit too fast, organizing production line work teams and restructuring management at the same time. Others have had a better go. Major accomplishments are in evidence at Martin Marietta, Aerojet General, Harris, Westinghouse, Boeing, and Rockwell International.

On the commercial electronics side, Motorola has remained a star. A measure of the organization's commitment is evidenced by the almost $30 million spent each year in quality training programs for its employees. Is Motorola saving money as a result of decreasing defects and inspection requirements?

Try $700 million saved in 1991 (Smith 1991, 56). In 1988, Motorola won the Baldrige Award.

Detroit also joined the congregation in the 1980s. Ford was the first, followed by Chrysler and General Motors. The successful "Team Taurus" is a case in point, as are Chrysler's mini-van and recently unveiled 1993 LH car, GM's Tennessee-based Saturn plant, and, of course, Cadillac.

Unfortunately, these efforts were often characterized by free-standing operations or in costly "skunk works," typically set up at remote sites to escape from the tinkering of top management and entrenched constituencies (*Los Angeles Times,* a 1992).

Without the total commitment of top management, Detroit doggedly endures with isolated streaks toward embracing the quality movement. It's a lot easier when the top dog joins the puppies.

Thousands of examples exist at county and local levels. Representative is Charlotte County, N.C. County administrator Tom Frame recently organized the hiring of the consulting firm, Qualtec, a subsidiary of Florida Power and Light, to provide seminars for employees at all levels on the improvement of services through teamwork (*Charlotte Sun Herald* 1992). Frame sold the project by giving his own presentation to the county commissioners that included presentations by personnel from Florida Power and Light and from St. Joseph's Hospital. Both organizations have impressive records in quality management based on the Deming philosophy.

Examples can fill tomes bigger than the one handed to Churchill, but the flavor remains distinct. We are at a dynamic point in a recognizable sequence of events.

The origins and maturation of modern quality can plausibly be summed up in three names: Watt, Ford, and Deming. The connections can also be simply articulated: machines, mass production, and getting it right.

PART 2 | THE FOURTEEN POINTS

■ The most popular edifice of the "new" quality is constructed on Deming's Fourteen Points, which are summarized below. There is considerable overlap among the points. Because they are not mutually exclusive, Deming's book, *Out of the Crisis,* dances freely from the reinforcement of one point to another. Admittedly, it is difficult to discuss the application of one point without touching on another. Deming's book, however, is a vastly important work and well worth serious study as well as constant use as a reference. It is, after all, a vital repository of the faith.

1. Create Constancy of Purpose Toward Improvement of Product and Service

A central problem with U.S. management in both public and private arenas is it's detrimental focus on the near-term. Near-term problems, such as profits, shareholders, public relations, getting reelected, and so on are real and important issues. Dealing with these issues, however, is not nearly as important as the very existence of the organization over the long pull.

Constancy of purpose involves the innovative allocation of resources toward long-term planning, research, and education and constant improvement in the design of products and services. The fundamental role of any organization must be to stay in business by providing goods and services beneficial to people—beneficial because they provide quality, continuity of employment, and pride in workmanship.

2. Adopt the New Philosophy

Deming tells us that American management is beset with lethal ailments. We are hung over with managers who found their ways to the top during the 1950s and 1960s, when the United States held the world market. As a result, we commonly accept levels of mistakes, inadequate training, antiquated supervision, job hopping, cost overruns, reactive planning, damage control, late and inadequate services, and dissatisfaction in the workplace.

We need a new mind-set in which passive acceptance is no longer tolerated. More than mere lip service, we need managers who *embrace* the new religion with a passion.

Example: You run a hamburger and hot dog stand at a marina. The annual community Fourth of July parade ends right in front of your store at noon. You pride yourself in your quality and service. You have always advertised the best quality meat—less than 25-percent fat. It has paid off. People routinely come to your place for a "real" hamburger. On July 3 you get your meat shipment. Somebody goofed. The hamburger meat has 30-percent fat. If you're a lip server to quality, you sell the hamburgers on the fourth. If you have a passion for quality, you put a sign up apologizing and just sell the hot dogs—you would not dream of doing anything else.

3. Cease Reliance on Mass Inspection to Achieve Quality

Relying solely on inspection to achieve quality is the same as planning for defects. Attaining quality through inspection in effect pays workers to produce faulty items and then pays others to correct the defects. Dr. Thomas Boardman has referred to inspection as akin to "harvesting," in the sense that it seeks to cull the satisfactory product *after* it is produced (Boardman 1992). Alternatively, statistical inspection of small samples with the goal of improving internal processes as well as improving supplier quality is a must. But the goal is to constantly reduce even this need. Quality is not produced after the fact; it is a result of never-ending improvements in the entire "system."

4. End the Practice of Awarding Business on the Basis of Price Tag

Price does not mean quality. It never did. Further, managers need to train and instruct their purchasing managers to work toward reducing the number of suppliers on the basis of quality alone. While two or more suppliers can meet "specifications" for parts, it does not mean that tolerances within that specification may not vary and that one part functions better in the final system than an "identical" part from another supplier. Organizations deeply committed to quality are in bed with their suppliers. It's a big bed—large enough to accommodate the supplier(s), design engineering, purchasing, manufacturing, services, sales, and everybody else. Seek long-term commitments and intimate trust with suppliers. Also note that two

24

shipping points from the same supplier can be as bad as two suppliers.

5. Improve Constantly and Forever the System of Production and Service

Improving quality is a never-ending cyclic enterprise. Continual improvement is forever necessary in every facet of procurement, marketing, design, customer support, administration, sales, training, finance, and every other activity. The concept is embodied in the Shewhart Cycle—the so-called PDCA Cycle, consisting of Plan, Do, Check, and Act. (The Japanese call it the Deming Cycle.) In the planning phase, a quality team addresses issues such as:

- What could be the most meaningful contributions of the team?

- What positive changes are needed?

- What existing information is available?

- Is new data required? If it is, what is the plan for acquiring it and how will it be used?

The Do phase executes the change or test, preferably on a small scale. The Check phase *measures* the outcome, and the Act phase either implements the change on a larger scale or reverts to making a better plan to accomplish the desired end. In all cases, the cycle continues with new applications or refinements of old applications. It never ends. Never.

6. Institute Training

The approach to training requires total revamping. Simple integration into existing training programs is not sufficient. Top management needs training to understand that the satisfaction of internal and external customers is a central quality issue. Middle management needs training to understand their role in distributing authority. Workers need training beyond learning their jobs from fellow workers. Quality programs cannot be implemented without extensive training, which results in a total re-think on the part of everyone.

7. Institute Leadership

Leadership involves setting well-defined strategic goals, with the understanding that the best people to devise effective methods of implementing those goals are the workers themselves. Leaders are more than simple bosses giving orders. They are team members who facilitate the building of people through their ability to listen, build consensus, and move positively toward common goals.

Still, leaders throughout an organization must have strong backgrounds in the work for which they are responsible. Without this capacity, much of our supervision degrades to dealing with numbers and not with process, because they don't understand the process. The problem is easily compounded through levels of "management" reporting. Leaders at every level must be trained and empowered to inform their superiors of changes that need to take place without fear. Leaders don't punish people; they bring out the best in people by providing an opportunity to contribute. Leaders don't simply supervise; they lead.

8. Drive Out Fear

None of us in the workplace is free to express ideas or offer suggestions unless we are secure. Deming points out that both *se* and *cure* come from Latin, meaning *without* and *fear,* respectively. Secure literally means without fear. There is a great deal of fear in the U.S. workplace. We are constantly bombarded by the quest for scapegoats in our businesses, institutions, and politics. Stick your face out and you could be next. They are weeded out and fired. From the shuttle's O-rings to Chicago's leaking tunnels, our managements point-and-shoot philosophy finds the bad guys in the face of adversity and simply eliminates them. We avoid making waves because of fear. We tolerate quotas and periodic reviews because of fear, practices that in turn generate fear. The loss in performance and the padded figures that result in our workplaces because of fear can only be characterized as astounding. Worst of all managers' fear most the quality movement itself, because it requires at the outset renouncing an autocratic, all-knowing posture. It requires a problem-directed, team-oriented humility.

9. Break Down Barriers Between Departments

Teamwork across internal company structures is a necessity. Common, almost axiomatic, in U.S. organizations are separate departments that naturally optimize their functions in accordance with their narrowly perceived, isolated missions. Relationships within organizations are often adversarial, conflicting, and oversimplified. For example, cost of warranty is typically blamed on manufacturing, when in fact any number of factors may contribute, such as original parts (suppliers), improper statistical control, a rush to production, false or misleading advertising, padded figures, and so on. *Another example:* Manufacturing and sales traditionally like high inventories to keep the line going and to respond to customers' wishes in a timely manner, while management extols the cost-saving advantages of low inventories.

Highly compartmentalized organizations that do not interact are not capable of implementing change that crosses functional boundaries of responsibility. Not long ago, an employee in a federal agency told me she had gone to her supervisor with an idea on how to integrate scheduling within the agency. She saw scheduling as a single, generic function. She was told to talk to the scheduling people in another section. The immediate reaction was, "Our problems are really quite different. I don't think that would work here." Her supervisor thought he did the right thing in directing her inquiry. Instead of organizing an inter-departmental effort, he simply passed her to a group with their own agenda. "I was really amazed," she said to me, "it was simply a matter of Not Invented Here. And I work for a company that has been 'implementing' TQM for over a year."

Compartmentalization builds turf, and turf builds barriers—my sand box and your sand box. She observed no system-wide organizational priorities—only priorities of sections and divisions—and no higher-level sense of organizational mission. In such a setting, nothing can happen until the walls come tumbling down, and the music can only be played by the lead trumpet.

10. Eliminate Slogans, Exhortations, and Targets for the Work Force

Charts and slogans themselves do not address the system. "Do it Right the First Time" is impossible if the worker is dealing with defective parts or machinery or inadequate statistical control. "Getting Better Together" cannot happen if no one will listen to your problems or suggestions. "Zero Defects" is not the responsibility of workers who cannot control the process in which they are embedded. Slogans are typically directed at the wrong people. Some may have a temporary effect, but for the most part are recognized as hoaxes. Management needs to learn that they are mainly responsible for im-

28

proving the system by removing common causes detected by statistical methods (Deming 1982, 67).

11a. Eliminate Numerical Quotas for the Work Force

Quotas are directed toward worker behavior and not toward an understanding of system process. Activity rates for workers are typically set at an average value. Consequently, half of the workers are better than the average, and half cannot keep up. The ones that are better slow down near the end of the day. The ones who are not as fast sacrifice quality for the speed needed to meet numbers. Quotas guarantee inefficiency and loss of quality. People meet quotas at any cost, whether they are associated with production or delivering services. They have to keep their jobs. Quotas are demoralizing. People don't want to stand around or engage in shoddy workmanship. Quotas treat people like machines and rob them of their right to individual pride of workmanship.

11b. Eliminate Management by Objectives

Management by Objective (MOB) goals (e.g., increase sales by 15 percent next year; decrease warranty costs by 10 percent; cut costs by 10 percent; improve productivity by 5 percent) are examples of quotas and don't work for at least two reasons. The first is the tendency of subordinates to find clever ways to meet the required numbers. It is easy to decrease the number of warranties by associating a second problem with an earlier one. All it takes is creative paperwork. Clever employees can achieve almost any objective and do so at the expense of quality. So can our federal government, which constantly plays with numerology to improve indexes and the paper shifting of funds to improve deficits. The second reason is that you can never achieve a goal that is outside of the envelope of the natural statistical variation of a system, without changing the system. A goal that is beyond the inherent capability of a system will not be reached. Setting simplistic goals without understanding the process and a specific plan to influence that process sets the focus in the wrong place—the end instead of the means.

12a. Remove Barriers that Rob Hourly Workers of Their Right to Pride in Workmanship

The inherent abilities of our people are largely wasted. Hourly workers are routinely faced with barriers to productivity. These include not only the setting of quotas, but lack of training, unwillingness of foremen to listen to and deal with problems, inadequate tools, supervisor turnover, and the clearly outdated mentality of mangers that treats the hourly worker as a commodity.

12b. Remove Barriers that Rob Management and Engineering of Their Right to Pride in Workmanship

Performance evaluations, merit ratings, and annual reviews are all detriments to pride in workmanship. Examples are evaluations on the basis of number of meetings attended by federal mediators, number of contracts negotiated, number of products developed in research, number of courses taken for self-improvement, number of papers published, and so on. It is a fallacy to rank order reward structures for next year based on what happened last year. Annual reviews foster competition, fear of losing credit, and a concentration on the quest to attain a good short-term rating as an individual and not as a team member. It is better to encourage a teamwork atmosphere, where groups, rather than individuals, are motivated to succeed. Employees should be paid on the basis of their experience and responsibilities over a period of time rather than simply being ranked according to short-term variation and circumstance.

13. Institute a Vigorous Program of Education and Self-improvement

The days are past when one can expect to attain a specific level of skill and simply execute those skills for the rest of one's career. We are in a dynamic, technological age, where education and increased knowledge are at a premium. The shortage we suffer is not so much a shortage of willing people, but a shortage of knowledge. There is a distinction between Point 6 and Point 13. Point 6 refers to the basis for training management and new employees. Point 13 refers to the need for continual education and self-improvement for everyone on the job (Deming 1982, 53).

14. Put Everybody to Work to Accomplish the Transformation

Everyone in the organization must be involved. Massive training is required to instill the courage to break with tradition. Every activity and every job is a part of the process.

There you have it. The Deming ideological envelope for the realization of quality. The onus for "building in" quality falls on top management, the distribution of power, the involvement of all personnel, complete re-training at every level, and the establishment of a single, coordinated organizational vision: quality.

THE NEW

PART 3 | QUALITY IN

ACTION

■ The Fourteen Points provide an ideological base. However, realizing quality takes more than grasping a set of principles. Next there has to be understanding. Understanding can be greatly enhanced by experience. What follows are glimpses of both good and bad experiences. The discussion is structured around four main components. These are:

- Building in quality

- Management

- Workers

- Training

Of course, all facets of the subject matter are inherently intertwined. Achieving system-wide quality requires diligent attention to all four interrelated components.

Building in quality focuses on the measurement and constant improvement of process, with regard to suppliers, internal organizational activities, and an enlarged concept of the customer community.

Management deals with the traumatic transformation that top and middle managers must face when implementing any serious quality movement.

The workers section stresses prevailing attitudes toward exercising power over subordinates at all levels and the virtues of true leadership through employee empowerment.

Training emphasizes the valuable returns to be realized with thorough training and retraining at any cost.

BUILDING IN QUALITY

The "new" quality extends far beyond concepts of quality control through inspection. Inspection inherently accepts the after-the-fact concession that products and services will naturally and always have defects. The broader approach to building in quality assaults this premise in three major ways. The combination of the three seeks to greatly diminish and, in some cases, even eliminate the need for inspection itself.

The first deals with the analysis and constant improvement of the process within an organization itself that provides either goods or services.

The second addresses the impacts of functions upstream of the internal process, mainly those of suppliers to the process.

The third turns to issues downstream of the internal process, such as distribution and end customer satisfaction.

The entire quality issue is viewed within the context of a complete system process, ala Sarasohn. Because it is the focal point to the beginning of quality implementation, we shall start with Deming's views on process.

Process

Among all else, Deming is an heroic teacher. During his seminars he routinely conducts a simple exercise to prove that it is a mistake to embrace the widely held concept that workers alone are accountable for the quality of their products and services.

The exercise is compelling. He selects a number of people from the audience to function as "workers" and an additional three to fill the role of "inspectors." The equipment to be used by the workers includes two containers, one larger than the other. The larger one contains 4,000 beads, of which 3,200 are white and 800 are red. The workers are also provided with a rectangular paddle that has 50 holes in it. Each hole is slightly smaller than a bead so that a single bead can rest in each recess. The workers are to "produce" white beads.

The production process begins with the pouring of the beads from the larger container into the smaller one, and then pouring them back into the larger container. The beads are thus mixed. The next step is to insert the paddle into the large container of beads and to shuffle it back and forth, so as to fill each of the 50 holes with one bead.

Deming goes through an extravagant and entertaining process of "training" his workers. He demands that the containers be tilted a certain way when pouring the beads and that the paddle consistently be inserted at a specific angle and agitated in a definite way. He checks their attempts and constantly cajoles them to improve on the process. His workers begin to understand the procedures for which there are to be no departures. "We know our business here," chides foreman Deming. After much demeaning wrath and fuss with regard to exact process, the workers are at last "highly trained." Production begins.

The output of the workers must now be closely monitored and, if their work does not meet management standards, they must be corrected. As each worker successfully extracts 50 beads, they move to the location of the inspectors and present their paddles. The first inspector counts the number of white beads and the number of red beads. The second inspector performs the same count, and the third inspector checks the two counts for consistency. Quality is a top priority of management.

The first worker produces 4 red beads. The second worker produces 5 red beads and is instructed to go back and concentrate on improving the process. The third worker produces only 3 red beads and is in line for a merit raise. The process continues through all the workers and is repeated again on successive days. In a later round, the third worker produces 8 red beads, and management concludes that worker number three is slipping. If the best worker can produce only 3 red beads, why can't the others? Clearly, more training is needed, or incentives should be raised. Periodic performance reviews result in the ranking of the workers, which in turn results in management decisions regarding who should get the most money, who should be let go, and who should be in line for promotion.

When the demonstration is concluded, Deming plots the results and shows clearly what everyone anticipates. The variation observed is due solely to statistical variation inherent in the random selection of red and white beads, given the population of each (i.e., the system). The limits of worker performance, no matter how willing or well trained the workers are, are determined by the system in which they are embedded. The system is statistically stable and cannot be changed by any management policy directed toward worker behavior related to job descriptions. Worker performance cannot be influenced by incentives, slogans, reviews, the "after-the-fact" quality control team, or anything other such strategy devised by management.

There are obvious ways to improve quality in this setting, such as improving the performance of suppliers or including the extraction of red balls as part of the work description. Solutions occur to the workers, but they are not empowered to suggest them. Their intellects are absorbed in concentrating on the mechanics of their specific job descriptions. Deming, as foreman, makes sure they stick to the details of their tasks in accordance with their training: "You're pouring the beads too fast," "Hold the paddle tighter," "You're not agitating correctly—slower, slower." They are willing and want to succeed, but are motivated by fear inherent in the system and competition among themselves. They are mechanical. Their intellects are destroyed.

Like the conventional British miner, the worker is trapped. Clearly, the production process is outside of the workers' control, but it is not outside the control of management. Only management can make the needed changes to improve quality. But managers cannot make such changes if they don't understand the process to begin with.

Enter Deming's use of Statistical Process Control.

Among Deming's more stellar contributions to quality management is the practical use by front-line workers of process control charts to determine the statistical stability of any process in question. The Deming charts effectively apply the concepts of Statistical Process Control and draw heavily on his pioneering work in this field during his employment with the Census Bureau in the 1940s. While the concepts are familiar to us today, it was Deming who had the vision and trust to train workers on their value and use. And because they are involved, the workers absolutely love it.

Consider the following example of a process control chart and its use. The example will be independent of any particular process. It could be the measurement of the length of ingots on a production line, the number of customer complaints, the number of defects, time spent waiting in line, the number of memos generated—anything at all.

We begin by taking a number of samples of the process we wish to measure. Each sample consists of a number of measurements. In this example, each sample consists of five measurements. The mean value of the measurements in each sample is calculated and tabulated. Samples are taken continuously through time to maintain a recurring measurement of the process. Table 3-1 shows the tabulation of the first ten samples in our example. As the number of samples increases, the statistics, of course, become more reliable.

The mean values for each sample are next plotted on a process control chart. The plot for our first ten mean values is shown in Figure 3-1.

Control limits are established to assist in determining the stability of the process. One simple determination of an upper control limit (UCL) and a lower control limit (LCL) can be based on the standard deviation of the mean values. A detailed account of established methods for determining UCLs and LCLs is given by Fabrycky (Fabrycky and Blanchard 1990, 305). In our example, we initially set the UCL at 11.6 and the LCL at 9.4.

When control limits are exceeded, the reason should be determined immediately. Since control limits are statistically derived, there is always a probability that individual measurements may fall outside of the control limits by chance alone. There is also the possibility that the system is statistically stable and that the control limits have been set too narrowly.

The Deming approach advocates the association of data that exceeds control limits, with one of two possible cause catego-

TABLE 3-1   Process Measurement Example

Sample Number	Value 1	Value 2	Value 3	Value 4	Value 5	Mean Value
1	10.1	8.2	9.6	10.5	9.9	9.7
2	11.2	10.5	8.3	9.2	10.6	10.0
3	8.1	11.5	9.4	9.9	8.3	9.4
4	12.6	12.2	13.5	12.9	14.0	13.0
5	8.3	9.4	7.9	11.0	12.2	9.8
6	11.7	9.3	10.2	8.9	9.7	10.0
7	9.8	11.5	10.5	11.1	10.2	10.6
8	11.2	12.3	10.4	9.9	11.7	11.1
9	10.4	9.2	10.0	8.6	9.1	9.5
10	10.9	11.5	12.7	11.8	10.7	11.5
. . . etc.						

NOTE   The mean of the means = 10.5
The standard deviation of the means = 1.1

ries. These are special causes and common causes. Special causes are due to transient events, such as a change in weather, use of a different fuel, or a particular worker's illness. Common causes are due to inherent properties of the system itself. Common causes can be fixed only by management.

When a control limit is exceeded, the analysis should begin with a search for a special cause. It is not always simple to ascertain the difference. Were the recent riots in Los Angeles due to the outcome of a single trial (special cause) or to a more

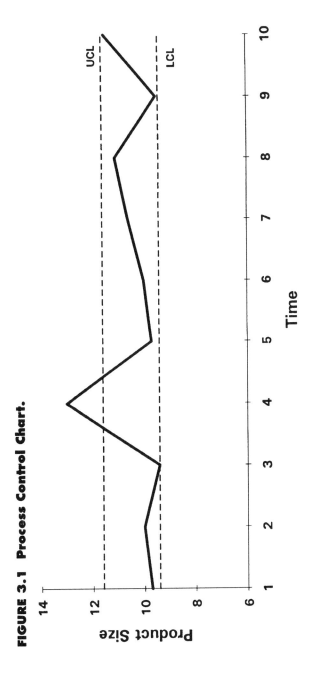

FIGURE 3.1 Process Control Chart.

fundamental, ongoing social problem in our cities (common cause)? Is the cause of an automobile recall due to careless workmanship, or is it due to the system that produced it? While is it wise to search for the special cause first, it is estimated that 95 percent of control limit deviations are due to common causes inherent in the system and that only 5 percent are special in origin.

In stable systems, the question automatically arises as to whether the control limits are set too widely. It is always wise to constantly identify the causes of variances, take action to reduce them, and tighten up the control limits to further improve quality. In fact, this is the manner in which Deming's advocates employ process charts in a never-ending quest to improve quality. It is never wise, however, to assume that the reason for excessive variance in a stable system is due to the workers alone. The workers can't control the variance in a stable system—only management can, by changing the system.

There is an interesting parallel between the profound simplicity of the process control chart and the emerging theory of Chaos, so clearly explained to us by James Gleick (Gleick 1987). The theory of Chaos accepts that there is a natural envelope of behavior in nature within which randomness abounds. For centuries, scientists and engineers have generated mathematical models of natural processes and then tried to explain why data did not always fit their deterministic equations. The ideas behind Chaos provide a different slant.

Observations of patterns in weather, animal populations, cotton prices, chromosomes, magnetic fields, galactic orbits, dripping faucets, and even the experiments themselves that scientists conduct clearly support the contention that there exists a natural variance around our simple linear models. In all cases the variance rambles within deterministic upper and lower limits. Chaos suggests that it may only be possible to make predictions within boundaries based on measures of variance of a process itself. Inside the boundaries, it cannot be said exactly what will happen next. The traditional approach in science has been to explain observed variance as a combination of factors such as incomplete data, or the need for refinement of parameters, or still unknown influences that affect the validity of our rigid equations. The theory of Chaos expects this behavior to be a natural condition of nature. Clouds are organized within well-defined envelopes, but they are always different.

Shewhart and Deming have simply found and applied the existence of Chaos in the production and service industry environments. Deming's stable process can no more be corrected by workers than a natural event. The weather cannot be changed by rewarding weather forecasters for good weather, decreasing their wages for bad weather, or putting them through annual reviews. They simply do not control the system.

Still, the idea that individual accountability is a primary ingredient in attaining quality remains rampant in our culture. One U.S. government bulletin embraces the following philosophy:

> The importance of the concept of accountability of individuals, and the power of a persuasive human knowledge among the workers, supervisors, managers and that each individual will be held accountable for his work products cannot be over stressed. Audit trails must be maintained that document completed work and the supervisors responsible for such work. People generally want to do the right thing, but in a large organization they frequently don't really understand what is the right thing. . . We should intensively and analytically evaluate how to handle compliance (holding workmen, supervisors and managers accountable) and to deal with failure in a manner that will have the highest payoff in improving quality and productivity.

Demingites call this frightening stuff. They are adamant about the folly that managers engage in when placing the emphasis of quality management on individual accountability. The folly manifests itself in the employment of incentives, quotas, rewards, reviews, slogans, and "one-liner" corporate goals as a sole means to influence worker performance that is taking place within an envelope of natural variance determined by the system. Deming and his legions are not impressed with the typical U.S. manager.

They also demonically demean the related central absurdity of simplistic MBO. The problem, they say, with Peter Drucker's MBO is that it focuses on goals and not on process.

The MBO numbers game perhaps reached its pinnacle in the United States during the short but debilitating Robert McNamara era at the Ford Motor Company. During that time, Ford management was dominated by accountants, so management was simple. It had to do with money! The quality of automobiles was completely subordinate to the management objective of increasing profits by cutting costs.

The Pinto disaster exemplifies the thinking. The Pinto had a lethal gas tank problem. The Ford Whiz Kids employed a method of cost-benefit analysis that calculated the cost of a human life at $200,725. The engineering solution to avoid future deaths due to burning was calculated at $137,000,000. The total cost of deaths and car damages without improvements were then costed at $49,500,000. The cost-benefit analysis clearly indicated that the Pinto should be left just as it was. It was. That's why you don't see them anymore.

In the 1980s, Ford began to seriously implement the concept that long-term quality was more important than short-term profit. The change was awesome. Ford began to embrace quality. Executives were no longer chastised for making errors.

The new Ford organization began to understand process. Top managers removed the old centralized simplistic directives and a lot of fear from the workplace. They also devoted monumental effort to the understanding of their customers and implemented substantial improvements in their supplier network. Among the outcomes were the highly successful Taurus and the Sable. The Ford Motor Company did a one-eighty. Instead of losing billions, their profit soared to nearly $6 billion per year.

The understanding of process is a central doctrine of the Deming approach. It is a difficult posture for the U.S. manager, both in and out of government, to assume. It requires a thorough mental turnaround through the acceptance of the idea that the process being managed may not be completely understood. Rather than sit in isolated offices employing management techniques born of the industrial revolution, managers must suddenly now relinquish their omnipotence and base their actions upon the realities of the process occurring beneath their very seats. The inherent admission on the part of management that not all is known about what happens beneath them or that one's career in management may have been better spent is not a funny one.

On the other hand, for all of us, what's going on in Japan and, to an increasing extent, in Germany versus U.S. federal and state governments and industries isn't so funny either.

Clearly, the majority of our managers face the responsibility of suffering a tough transition. The transition begins with understanding that they may not have complete access to hard measures related to everything they are supposed to understand and control. Like the lowly workers, U.S. managers are too commonly trapped in isolation by their own organizational structures and wind up giving direction but running nothing or, worse, by instituting shallow and destructive change. The transition must continue with an effort to quantify and understand the statistical stability of the processes that they manage, to positively empower the worker in the identification and solution of problems, and, above all, to come to understand that the issue of implementing true quality enhancement lies solely with them.

The measurement and careful analysis of process (i.e., what is actually happening) is the key to developing meaningful strategies aimed at improving quality. Therein lies the starting point. But it is only the starting point. It leads logically to specific designs for extending team involvement upstream to suppliers and downstream to the customers—the total end-to-end process.

All of this must be very difficult because not enough of us are doing it.

The Path Upstream

Quality management has traditionally been oriented around an after-the-fact measurement of the outcome of a process. In this scheme, the concept of a certain number of defects is inherently accepted. The aggressive Deming approach to quality management moves beyond this limited area in both directions. The path upstream from the simple acceptance of defects not only includes the analysis and continual improvement of internal process, but also logically extends to the intimate involvement of suppliers.

Less red beads coming in the door means more white beads going out the door.

A common practice for U.S. industry and governments at all levels has long been to maintain relationships with more suppliers than are actually needed. A major rationale for this convention has to do with simple security. Suppliers have a way of coming and going or of emphasizing the needs of other customers, as demands dictate. If you commit to only a few suppliers, how do you know they will always be there?

A second component of the security issue has to do with the

46

unwillingness of organizations to overexpose the details of what they are doing. Providing suppliers with too much information may render an organization vulnerable to the supplier offering the organization's proprietary innovations to competitors. Both of these strategies are based on fear.

Among the many impacts that Deming made at the General Motors Buick-Oldsmobile-Cadillac organization in the early 1980s was to eliminate these fears in the interest of a higher goal: quality.

The setting was in place. The introduction of the Quad 4 engine at GM provided a unique opportunity to acquire new equipment and a new plant. It also offered an opportunity to apply Deming's concepts regarding the virtues to be gained from a higher level of involvement with a reduced number of suppliers.

Purchasing was enlisted to lead the way through intensive team involvement. Team members combed the world for potential suppliers. The members independently wrote their assessments of engine part suppliers. They were limited to eight candidates each. Further team reviews were conducted to bring the number of suppliers for each part to one—a well-known (though not widely followed) Deming goal. In place of the traditional competitive bidding approach, GM strove to develop long-term relationships with willing suppliers and went so far as to enlist them to play an active role in designing parts, in order to enhance manufacturability and quality. The Quad 4 program wound up with 74 suppliers, as opposed to the usual number of over 200 for GM engines. From this and other company-wide team efforts, the Cadillac came back.

Across town, Team Taurus also dropped the old Ford low bidder approach (Peters 1988, 212). The team sought out its highest-quality suppliers and involved them in the early stages of design. The subframe supplier, A. O. Smith of Milwaukee, became so involved with Team Taurus that it began using its own drafting department to draw up subframe specifications for Ford's approval. Team Taurus spread the philosophy among all suppliers, including those for lighting, plastics, and carpets. Innovation abounded with attention to details never before considered. Secrets took a back seat to a single, pervasive ambition: quality. Taurus and the Ford Motor Company won big.

The scenario is not limited to Detroit. H. Harrington tells us how supplier partnerships played a role at IBM (Peters 1988, 81):

> In the 1970's we made the mistake of talking to our suppliers in terms of AQLs (Acceptable Quality Levels) when we should have been talking parts per million. I am convinced that if in the 1970's we had been talking parts per million, today we would be talking parts per billion.

In the short span of time from 1980 to 1983, IBM's defects in parts per million for transistors fell from 2,800 to 200 (an improvement in quality by a factor of 140). Defects in transformers fell from 4,200 to 100 per million (an improvement in quality by a factor of 42), and defects in capacitors fell from 9,300 to 80 per million (an improvement in quality by a factor of 116) (Peters 1988, 82).

The Procter & Gamble Company took similar strides in breaking down traditional barriers with its suppliers after meeting up with Deming in 1986. Profit margins were slowly declining. Interestingly, P&G looked not only at the quality of their products, but also at the quality of their advertising and distribution. Rather than react by streamlining costs through Management By Objective, or by implementing some other blind reactive approach, they simply took a hard look at the spectrum of their own processes.

Among their efforts to review relationships with suppliers, P&G management took a deep look at the process involved in working with its advertising agencies. They also did some research on the effectiveness of advertising campaigns. To their chagrin, they found an incredibly complex procedure for campaign prototype and storyboard production and review. To make things worse, their research proved that only 20 percent of their advertising was effective. The other 80 percent did nothing but cost money.

P&G set about instructing the agencies on their new-found Deming philosophy. Cross-corporate teams were formed. For the first time, P&G opened up their vast store of market research data that they had never before shared with agencies— or with anyone else. They set aside their ingrained fear of "leaks" reaching the competition in favor of providing the copywriters with highly prized information to assist them in effectively targeting the customers.

The management at P&G threw corporate fear of being wrong to the breeze. They also picked up on a few other convictions of the modern quality creed. For example, they took a new view on the ranking of personnel. P&G's manager of corporate quality, Earl Conway, adopted the philosophy that ranking focuses on the wrong thing. Ranking, it was decided, is prone to error because it simplistically assumes that workers are totally responsible for what they do. The focus should be on the system in which they are embedded and not the workers alone.

How does P&G feel about the costs for all of this? P&G management used to talk about a choice between quality and cost, believing that quality came with a price tag. What they discovered was that the proper application of total quality principles, in fact, simultaneously improved quality as well as flexibility and response time and that all of this tied into reduced costs. It was a major paradigm shift.

P&G is happy with the new mind-set—pleased enough to continue to expand their efforts, both upstream and downstream. The reason that team involvement works so well with suppliers is the same reason that composite miners do better than conventional miners—and are happier doing it. People flourish when they are asked to and then allowed to.

The Path Downstream

Tom Peters is prolific in bestowing gems upon us. During a July 1991 airing of the Public Broadcasting Systems's Nightly Business Report, he offered one in summation of exceptional merit.

"The customer," he said, "is the writer, director, and star of quality."

Demingites agree most emphatically that the customer is of paramount importance to the mind-set of everyone in an organization—that customer satisfaction is, in fact, the most critical element. Quality should always be directed toward the present and future needs of the consumer.

This philosophy is key to any long-term view. The cost of the disgruntled consumer is often invisible and difficult to assess. But it is known to be high. Ford estimates through their market research that unhappy customers are two and a half times more likely to tell their friends about their problems than happy customers are to relate their good stories. An integral part of Deming's philosophy is that profits are driven by loyal customers and not just satisfied customers.

But who are the customers/consumers? Clearly, one type of customer is the individual or organization that actually purchases goods or services from providers. While this includes retail consumers, the retailers, in turn, are customers of providers who are also, in turn, customers for their own suppliers of materials. But it goes further. Organizations themselves are complex combinations of internal customers and suppliers of information, goods, and services. Everyone in any organization can be viewed as both a supplier and a customer.

Suppliers provide products, services, and information, and customers provide feedback (i.e., requirements), either directly or indirectly. Ishikawa's total perspective is based on the importance of the role of the customer. The customer governs virtually all of his thinking.

But to Ishikawa, the "customer" is simply whoever receives your work, whether they be internal or external to an organization. He came to this realization after asking a group of workers in one section of a steel mill why they didn't visit workers in another section to determine how they might improve their output. The workers replied that they were unable to do that because the workers in the section they supplied would treat them as meddlers in their business, or, as Ishikawa put it, as "spies." Fear, again.

The extension of this supplier-customer relationship clearly opens up a vast set of opportunities for implementing quality improvements. Cadillac provides a case in point. In the late 1980s, the development process was decomposed into six categories, along the lines of a work breakdown structure.

The new realization at Cadillac was that, in addition to the external customer (the buyer), there are internal customers, such as design, materials, tooling, manufacturing, finance, assembly, distribution, and so on. Over 60 tailored improvement teams were put into place company wide. People at *all* levels were listened to and believed because quality, among other things, has to do with customer satisfaction. Between 1985 and 1988, Cadillac moved from a ranking of 16 to among the top 4 luxury cars.

Clearly, the organization and empowerment of internal customers (i.e., belief in the workers) is an important part of the quality equation—important because it has a direct effect on the quality of the external product or service.

Playmobil, a $200-million-dollar-a-year German toy company, has placed a proper and profitable emphasis on both. For the internal folk, they have built a new headquarters, designed to break down interior barriers. Designers, mold makers, salespeople, bookkeepers, and executives all have instant access to each other at the facility. They do a lot of sitting around and talking.

To keep in touch with the outside world, a "Playmobil Park" was opened in October 1990. The Park is now routinely visited by some 5,000 consumers each month. Professionally trained personnel watch and interact with the children. Mostly they just listen. They are aptly called "listeners."

The Playmobil management is totally focused on its ultimate customer—the child. Long ago they recognized that they faced a difficult problem—namely that toys for children are made by adults. In the meantime, buyers were focussing on technology. They wanted more motors, more electronics, and high-tech talking gadgets. But Playmobil took an utterly simplistic approach. They wanted to know more about what a child does with a toy. The quest became a 10-year commitment. That's what it took Hans Beck to come up with the simple and beautiful answer. It is not the toy that should do something—it is the children that do something with the toy.

Beck observed that children with a simple wooden car in which they could place and remove people, luggage, and so on, were much happier exploiting their imaginations than they were with a technological toy that did only one thing. Children are not passive observers. They are much more captivated when doing something with a toy rather than having a toy do something for them. The idea expanded to add-ons within a theme. Whole circuses, villages, and parks were created. Today, Playmobil doesn't sell to buyers who don't see the complete system concept—a concept that allows the child's imagination to glide off into hours of creative fun and, yes, want to add to their collections.

The people at Playmobil Village still listen to their real customers religiously and carry out the philosophy of their president, who believes that a product is not sold when it is bought by the consumer. It is sold when it is bought by the consumer and the consumer is satisfied. Until the customer is satisfied, it has not been sold.

Knowing what the customer wants takes a creative combination of market research and vision. Vision creates new markets. Deming is not enthralled with the long-term prospects of companies that measure progress solely on the basis of current or projected market share. One of his favorite observations is that no customer asked for electric lights, or photography, or the telephone.

Rational, another highly successful German company, owes its current status not only to an intimate knowledge of its customers' environment but also to an accurate vision of its customers needs. Rational makes ovens for professional chefs. They are a world class quality organization, with total downstream dedication. They have their own staff of chefs and customer engineers who travel the world showing up at customer installations, even when things are going great. The chefs also talk to the engineers back home. Together, they came up with a winner.

Rational invented a new oven with a complete spectrum of uses for the chef. The oven uses any combination of dry and steam heat for roasting, stewing, baking, or poaching—all in a compact space. After 8 years of perfecting the product, Rational management committed to their vision completely by abruptly discontinuing sales of their conventional convection ovens—a plumb that amounted to a mere 60 percent of their business! Everyone thought the boss was nuts. He wasn't.

In Landsburg, just west of Munich, manager Siegfried

Meister declares that profit is not the goal of their organization. Profit is a natural result of serving the customer. Serving the customer is the principal goal, not making money.

It's that way on the production floor too, where multiple copies of the same poster are in evidence. It reads:

Gut Genug? Der Kunde entscheidet!

In the United States it would read:

Good Enough? The Customer will decide.

Not everyone embraces the idea that customers decide. In the mid-1980s, General Motors elected to update and continue with the bulky Chevrolet Caprice. According to one industry analyst (*Los Angeles Times,* b 1992):

What they did was take the old Caprice, put it on a computer screen and wrap a new skin around it.

When asked to evaluate the new prototype, consumers thought it was ugly. But the GM designers loved it. GM had a choice to make. The final decision, based on money, was that design modification would simply cost too much. Besides, designers are supposed to know what consumers *really* want. After being introduced at the end of 1990, the new Caprice attained half of its projected sales in 1991. Sales in 1992 were even slower. One of two Caprice plants is among the 21 GM plants marked for shutdown by 1995.

The list of organizations that went through remarkable transformations when everyone began thinking "customer customer, customer" is impressive. In the 1980s, the Herco Company of Indianapolis, maker of machine tools, was playing the numbers game. Get it out the door no matter what the cost or what it looked like. The corporate philosophy? Screw it! Ship it!

Since then, Herco has accomplished a monumental turn-around by embracing the new quality ethic and a vision for product. Their market concentration is now on the smaller machine shop, with limited runs of parts. Cost and training are major factors with these smaller operators. The new Herco machine is programmable, easy to use, capable of quick recon-figuration, and affordable. A major feature is the "Ultimax" control console, which invokes a variety of operational and graphics software functions through a simple instruction set that requires minimal training.

Herco uses the term "value engineering" in their TQM program. Customer service is at a premium. The 1980s are over. The workers have pride. Everybody is in on it. Workers on the Herco floor understand that keeping the customer happy is imperative to keeping their own jobs. The spirit is evident everywhere—they're in for the long pull.

Building in quality is a system consideration. Throughout Deming's thunderings and warnings regarding process, suppli-ers, and customers, the emphasis is always toward optimizing the system. Optimization is achieved through cooperative em-powerment. Cooperation is achieved through a common focus on quality. The focus of all concerned is on quality of the system alone. Not on personalities. And not on power. That common ambition must be present in all relationships between manage-ment, unions, suppliers, customers, and workers. A simple, all-pervasive attitude that in the aggregate allows quality in action. Demingites profess that, if you defend yourself, you will lose. A better solution is for everyone to win.

MANAGEMENT

Fortunately (or unfortunately), middle managers and workers give a great deal of attention to the climate set by their bosses.

If the boss stresses finance, everyone stresses finance. If the boss likes certain words, everyone finds a way to use them in conversation. If the boss wears blue suits and red ties, more people start showing up for meetings in blue suits and red ties. And the boss's corporate strategy becomes everyone's corporate strategy, even if it's wrong.

People do this almost unconsciously because they want to succeed and because, quite simply, the person who resides at the very top of our vertically structured organizations, whether they provide goods or services, has incredible influence. It's called power.

Those that are personally confronted by Deming quickly discover that they may need to do something about any vision of omnipotence they may possess. David Kearns, chairman at Xerox, did not have a happy first meeting with the good Doctor. In short, they were told that they didn't really know what they were doing. Specifically, the focus was on short-term profits, customers were not really understood, direction was coming from the top down, and measurements were fear oriented. Most managers cannot tolerate such treatment. Fortunately for Xerox, Kearns was one of the best managers around. He knew in the early 1980s that his organization was on the way out of business and that cultural change was the only answer. Tinkering with the existing system would not hack it.

Kearns proved to be a leader in every sense of the word. He had the grit, the self-confidence, to change. He subsequently led Xerox through one the most exemplary quality-oriented transitions the country has seen.

The implementation of quality unquestionably requires dramatic upheaval in traditional management thinking. Our colleges, universities, institutions, and on-the-job experiences have all trained us to do something else. In this culture, quality takes a lot more than just an open mind. It takes a total jolt and a half throughout the entire management chain.

Lockheed California Company provides a good example of what it takes for management-wide training and the establishment of their version of Employee Participation Circles (EPCs). The EPCs are trained by referees (or what QC people call facilitators). A steering committee oversees and guides the EPCs. Up to 50 EPCs have been active at a given time, investigating specific quality issues dealing with departmental interactions—internal customers. The groups are formed and dissolved as well-defined assignments are identified and resolved. One employee reported to me that his 1 hour per week participation on an EPC team resulted in company savings of $100,000 per year. His reaction?

"I really felt good about that accomplishment. They actually listened to us and it worked. I felt valuable and I still do."

A happy miner, he.

At Lockheed, management made it possible. Interestingly, this same individual, later employed at a government aerospace center, was summarily rebuked by his immediate supervisor for suggesting that similar team meetings may be a method for identification and resolution of problems with their interdepartmental customers. The new employee, in an effort to bring his positive experience to his new environment, offered a series of proposals followed by responses, rebuttals, and more responses. His personal communication to me related the dialogue. It went like this:

PROPOSAL: *"During a Property Records Group staff meeting, I proposed that Property Records meet with the Property Control Group informally to discuss existing or potential problems. Both groups are within the same division. Such an action, I explained, would allow problems to be vocalized and resolutions brainstormed. Overall, this action would improve communications and understanding."*

RESPONSE: *I was informed that if an employee has a problem, the proper procedure is to elevate the problem to his or her supervisor. The supervisor would then voice the problem at the manager's staff meeting. It would be decided at the staff meeting whether or not the problem necessitated both groups meeting."*

Undaunted, the new employee persevered:

PROPOSAL: *"By following the response, the informality of open discussion between groups to identify problems would be lost. Plus, some people feel awkward bringing their problems to a supervisor that may be viewed as threatening."*

RESPONSE: *"Are you telling me that the existing procedure does not work?"*

The new employee now retreated. Fear came into the equation. Unfortunately for him, his past experience had been so favorable that he sought once again to open the issue through yet another proposal:

PROPOSAL: *Because both groups are unable to meet to discuss potential problems, I propose that a questionnaire be established and circulated to groups that we interact with. Such a questionnaire would be one page and general. Basically, the document would request statements of problems and ideas concerning our group functions and interactions. Overall, such an action would polish the group and be in support of TQM."*

RESPONSE: *I was reminded that the procedure concerning how a problem is formally elevated had been voiced and I was again trying to find fault with it. The proposed questionnaire would be acknowledging that problems exist within our group. Also, who would have time to create such a document? We are not a product or service industry, hence TQM would not apply here. I was told to direct my focus on my own job and not to be concerned with problems that pertain to the group as a whole."*

Now, clearly an adversary, the new employee buckled under.

"I told my boss I will keep my blinders on and no longer listen to problems voiced by other groups unless they pertain to my job, alone."

My once empowered friend is now back and buried in the "conventional" mine—and looking for a new job to boot. We may be depressed by his treatment, but we cannot blame his middle manager, who is simply living out his cultural heritage.

It is not at all surprising that the quality gurus continually stress the importance of direct participation of the top dog in any serious quality effort. W. E. Conway (President and Chief Executive of the Nashua Corporation) has had some of Deming rub off on him. In response to a request from an interested executive wishing to visit Nashua to learn more of their successful quality program, Conway simply told the hopeful visitor that, if you can't come, send nobody.

Donald Peterson, CEO and president of Ford, remembers how Deming stipulated that he would have to be the one to meet with him—not someone down the ladder.

The word is commitment, and it must begin at the top. This commitment includes the ability to assess and question the very process that is being managed, as well as the ability to do it without fear. This is a novel commitment that does not rely on scapegoats, such as demanding labor unions, high wages, shoddy workmanship, government restrictions, and cheap labor. It's a commitment that sets a tone of self-inquiry, openness, allowance for error, and the belief that what we need to do *we can do ourselves.* The commitment is made by managers who recognize the intimate end-to-end relationships between suppliers, workers, and consumers of goods and services as these affect quality management. Such a positive commitment acknowledges the dimensions of the "system." Such a commitment releases willing and waiting workers at all levels to achieve their highest capacities. This is the fabric from which the fervor for quality is fashioned. The top banana has to catch this feverish commitment.

Case in point—Fiero. As a result of the 1980 airing of the NBC documentary, *If Japan Can, Why Can't We?*, Dr. Deming was invited to Pontiac. The resulting impact on the development of the Fiero was substantial. All the ingredients were put into place. Statistical Process Control (SPC) tools were not only used in the production environment, but were also embraced within the organization's internal provider/customer relationships, including finance, employee relations, and even the tax department.

Close teamwork, conventionally alien to Detroit, between design, engineering, manufacturing, assembly, sales, marketing, and all aspects of development was established. Significantly, suppliers were involved in designs—some before contracts were even finalized. Worker classifications were reduced and responsibilities delegated. Worker allegiance and devotion to the new car flourished. The management culture shifted toward leadership through the understanding that, in the end, they were dealing with a diverse set of people with varying needs.

Fiero won awards: Best 1983 Design, American Car of the Year in 1984, and another rating among the Ten Best of 1984.

But Pontiac doesn't run General Motors. GM was hedging against a continual oil shortage into to 1980s, and the Fiero wound up with a decidedly un-zippy engine. The car also had a well-publicized fire problem. The Fiero team earnestly set about to correct these problems as well as to implement other features gleaned from customer feedback.

But GM's top management also found themselves in an internal struggle. Chevrolet had continually advocated the termination of the Fiero concept, fearing direct competition with the Corvette. Politicos throughout GM won. Pontiac was "re-organized," and the car was dropped by the end of 1988. Had the Fiero team been allowed to "improve constantly and forever" (Deming's Point 5), without the dictates of GM top management, the results would likely have been different. Fiero had anticipated the demand of Japanese sporty two-seaters that would shortly emerge. All was not lost, however, as many of the Pontiac people found their way to Buick, Oldsmobile, and Cadillac. In the late 1980s, Cadillac was already on the move.

Cadillac's Roseta M. Riley recounts the story (Riley 1992):

> We downsized in the gas crisis despite what customers said. We dropped to 16th. We were entrenched in traditional behavior with adversarial relations with our people. We instituted cultural change, a new focus on the customer and a disciplined approach to planning. We had no quality plan. The business plan *is* the quality plan. From 1985 to 1990 we came from 16th to 4th.

In 1985, they implemented "simultaneous engineering," involving cross-functional teams from engineering, manufacturing, suppliers, finance, and the United Auto Workers. A 2-year basic training program was instituted.

One team, the Recognition and Rewards Team, decided to eliminate rankings and employee appraisals, explaining that:

> One half is above average and the other half is below average. Tell people that they are average long enough and they will be. We don't have "average people" anymore—we have quality people.

In 1987, they formalized a "UAW/GM Quality Network," under which joint responsibility for quality was accepted by both the union and GM. Traditional adversaries became partners. One UAW part design saved a whopping $52 million. Cadillac turned the organization chart upside down. Managers stopped bossing and became leaders. As Riley puts it:

Management set strategic objectives and people decided how to get there.

"Design for Manufacturability" led to simpler design, ease of assembly, and reduction in variation. Among the results were a 70-percent reduction in customer problems, a 65-percent improvement in reliability and durability and a 1-year reduction in lead time.

When the Malcolm Baldrige Award people asked a 26-year veteran Cadillac worker how he liked his job, the answer was: "The first twenty years were awful. The last six have been fantastic."

Cadillac turned around because the bosses turned around. The turnaround set an atmosphere for the latent power of respect and teamwork to flourish.

The multidisciplinary team concept exemplified at Fiero and Cadillac is an integral component of the quality movement. The expanded team concept is catching on. It is now finding its way into conventional systems engineering practices in the form of additional key membership on what systems engineers have traditionally called the *system design team*. In the past, system design teams have customarily focused on hardware and software design throughout product development. An increasing number of development system design teams are now including marketing, production, suppliers, operations personnel, and customer representatives, in addition to simply hardware and software design personnel (Reilly 1993). When total teamwork flourishes among people of all departments, it is not surprising that traditional adversaries became compatriots.

Says consultant Michael Mescon, former Dean of Georgia State University Business School (*Star Free Press,* b 1992):

> Companies with a tradition of adversarial relationships—among people and departments—will have contentious bosses too. There, you'll have people and divisions trying to build prestige upon the ruins of each others failures.

The good news is that an increasing number of top managers, no matter what their age, are exhibiting the capacity for change. That faculty was clearly instrumental in the ability of Florida Power and Light to set their course—a course that would lead to the Deming Prize.

FP&L senior vice president Bud Hunter had good reason to be proud of his career. The company was widely viewed as a model to be emulated in the utility arena. When one of his managers visited Japan and returned extolling the new faith, Hunter was not convinced. When another did the same, he decided to go himself. It didn't take long for Hunter to realize that there were better ways of doing business. He came back very dissatisfied with his career. But he wasn't dissatisfied for long.

Hunter became the hunter, and FP&L began its quest for quality. The program was based on four axioms: Customer Satisfaction, Management by Fact, Respect for People, and Implementation of the Deming PDCA (Plan-Do-Check-Act) Cycle.

In keeping with the gospel, FP&L expanded the notion of customer to include anyone who received anyone else's work within the organization, as well as external consumers of services. Through market research, for example, they discovered that their external customers were happy with the low-power outage rates, but were unhappy with the time needed to repair any given outage. FP&L didn't know it till they asked. Through the enlistment of worker ideas and follow-up participation, they decreased outage time by 27 percent over the next 5 years. Management by Fact meant forgetting instinct and experience and finding out what was actually going on.

The Respect for People part included involving everyone in the organization in identifying areas for improvement through the formation of literally thousands of teams. People were instructed that no one would lose their job by being feisty and frank during their team efforts. Interestingly, extensive training was also directed toward middle management to orient them more toward mentoring as opposed to simply giving orders. Everybody listened to everybody.

The PDCA cycle, Plan-Do-Check-Act, was diligently applied and monitored, particularly in applying statistical measurement. The PDCA cycle, based on the Shewhart cycle, is comprised of six steps.

The first step involves defining the most important improvement that a given quality circle team can address. The definition includes delineation of what data is needed, how it may be obtained and analyzed, and a plan for action. The second step is to carry out the plan, preferably on a small scale at first. Step three entails observing the effects of the change or test. Step four is devoted to studying the results to determine what has been learned and what can be predicted. Step five repeats step one with the new-found knowledge. Step six repeats step two, and so on, until the issue is resolved. Through this cycle, a new level of stability of performance is reached.

It took diligence and perseverance, but FP&L went on to get the brass ring (i.e., Japan's Deming Prize). It could not have happened without the constancy of top management. Top manager Hunter turned out to be a true top manager.

The best intentions of upper and middle management, however, can often be thwarted by organizational structure. The needed ability to knock down barriers can be particularly difficult when the organization has inherently created toughly ingrained turf—that well-known malady that attacks organizations as they get old. There are two generic types of organizational structure: the *functional organization* and the *matrix organization*. In reality, the implementation of these generic structures involves a great diversity of expression. In some circumstances, one might find a mixing of these two organizational structures, depending on products or services. But turf is almost always involved.

The functional organization is organized around projects. The particular functions are determined by the mission of the organization, whether in government or in the marketplace. Each project structure repeats the necessary functions to achieve project goals, such as engineering, manufacturing, operations, and testing. The functional organization is basically fashioned for situations where products or services remain fairly stable over time, such as the automobile, steel, or home entertainment industries.

The functional organization tends to have more stability with regard to both project organization and personnel turnover from project to project. The functions may involve many disciplines, and the same disciplines can be repeated in different functional arms.

The basic matrix organization consists of permanent functional pools, such as an engineering pool, a manufacturing pool, and so on. The pools are tapped as needed for projects as they come and go. Matrix organizations are designed to deal with varying products or services, such as research or high-tech enterprises, where the work to be done is predisposed to change over relatively short periods of time. Project managers decide on who is needed and call upon the resources in various pools to provide the appropriate personnel from across the matrix.

The matrix concept is inclined to exhibit less conformity in project structures because project managers tend to have more freedom in the way they organize in adapting to projects of different natures. Also, it is generally easier for personnel to move from project to project in a matrix organization. Functional organizational structure tends to foster the creation of functional turf. The matrix organizational structure encourages the creation of discipline-oriented turf. And turf is a great ossifier.

There are, in fact, two manifestations of turf. One is horizontal. The other is vertical.

The horizontal turf problem arises when two different departments have overlapping or repetitive functions. When competition arises, a great deal of energy is expended by each department to justify their mini-empires.

Vertical turf is created by middle and upper managers who insist that the chain of communication follow a path upwards in one department, across to peers at some higher level, and then downward in another department. This infrastructure inherently creates barriers to communications between workers at lower levels who have common problems—and common solutions.

Are these problems real? Yes. The instances are bountiful. During the 1980s, the vertical turf problem alone destroyed a high-tech government communications system. The developers lived in one organizational structure, and the users lived in another. The communication path between them went upwards vertically to top technical management, across to technical peers, and downward vertically. Requirements were filtered and modified. Design decisions having little to do with real user needs were made at the top, and instructions were sent down. The real developers and the real users never had the benefit of meeting through a system design team. They didn't even know what each other looked like. Turf is opaque. Layers of turf are impenetrable. Ten years and $30 million dollars later, there was still no product. They continue to work today under organizational conditions that inherently corrupt any probability of success.

Whether the existing turf is functionally-oriented, discipline-oriented, horizontal, or vertical, the serious implementor of a quality program must always consider the means of eliminating interdepartmental self-interests. Reorganization may not always be necessary. It certainly will not, in itself, solve quality problems. But it may be a serious candidate for examination in concert with the total quality program. Like all quality issues, it is best addressed by a quality team of upper and middle managers and workers.

But, in the end, who is the only person who can reorganize? The one that has to start it all? Mr. or Ms. Numero Uno.

WORKERS

One of the most significant findings emerging from the Florida Power and Light quality effort was that employees, when given the chance, were more interested in achieving recognition for their roles as contributors to quality improvements than they were in making more money. FP&L is truly a model for eliminating barriers to experiencing joy and pride in work.

Not all people are happy in their work. It's all too easy to become mechanical in a mechanical environment. Why try harder if no one cares? You can't blame workers who are unmotivated and crushed by management.

Tom Peters once asked a woman on an elevator where she worked. She replied, "Fourteen."

That's where she got off.

Contrast that response with one from an electronic parts packer in a shipping department at Hewlett Packard. An ex-employee of HP, and now a colleague of mine, related to me what happened one day when she asked the parts packer where he worked. What followed was a 15-minute unilateral discourse explaining the computer-supported fault isolation techniques used by field engineers and how that translated into requests for specific parts to be shipped to specific locations in a timely manner. The packer related in detail how it was his responsibility to support the customer by getting the right parts to the right place at the right time without error. He walked her through the paces of receiving an order, getting the part, packaging it, and placing it in the right-sized box with appropriate protective filling. Next he made up the label and placed it on the box. Then he looked inside the box again to be sure the content was consistent with the order and the label. Next he held the box closed and shook it to be sure everything was safe. Then, and only then, did he close and seal the box.

"I do this very carefully, but without delay. If the right part doesn't get to the right place at the right time, the customer ain't happy. If the customer ain't happy, this organization is in trouble. It's very important that I don't make a mistake. I know there's a lot of people in this company, but if it doesn't happen right here, the whole thing isn't going to work. A lot depends on what I do right here. That's what I do."

Why does the HP worker give an answer that lasts a full 15 minutes and our friend on the elevator's first response to where she worked was location, not function? Simple. The woman who got off on the fourteenth floor works *for* a *boss*. The parts packer works *with* a *leader*.

The word is motivation. Motivation is quite simply and naturally given birth by an atmosphere that enables pride in workmanship, a sense of professionalism, and a feeling of importance. It's called self-respect.

The condition is gained by allowing individuals to gain self-respect. Perhaps the greatest compliment one can pay to another human being is to simply ask them a question. Asking workers how to do things better is an integral part of the quality movement. It simply does not occur to conventional managers to open up to line workers by asking them what they think about the way business is being conducted or if they have any ideas about how to improve. Quality is achieved by people for whom other people care. Demoralized robots aren't interested in quality.

What good comes to a production worker in making suggestions to a foreman if the foreman just smiles and walks away?

What good comes from filling out a report when something goes wrong, being told someone will look into it, and then nothing ever happens?

What good comes from having a foreman who winds up playing some numerical game because he or she knows nothing about the real job?

What good comes from high rates of absenteeism because workers view their jobs as something they do simply in return for wages and not as a source of pride and satisfaction?

What good is there in superintendents who are motivated to do nothing because there is no explanation required for not making waves?

What good is there in essentially ordering workers to build defectives with faulty factory equipment that has not been replaced in years?

All of these conditions are rampant in our workplaces. All workers ask for is a chance to do a good job, to take pride in their work, and to be proud of the company. That's not a whole lot. In the meantime, they can only do what they are asked to do under difficult conditions. This is not the breeding ground of quality.

But it's not just the folks at the bottom of our pyramids that suffer. The principle extends beyond the subject matter of factory workers. Unlike the miners who started showing up for work or the Lockheed employee who "felt valuable," too many workers and middle managers in the United States suffer under management that just hasn't quite got it yet. There is still a rampant and appalling inability to understand that people who are motivated to do something meaningful, in any walk of life, are motivated by their own vision of who they are and what they are contributing.

Self-respect and money are two different things. Two decades ago, R. H. Tawney wrote (*Los Angeles Times,* c 1992):

> Since even quite common men have souls, no increase in material wealth will compensate them for arrangements which insult their self-respect and impair their freedom. A reasonable estimate of economic organization must allow for the fact that, unless industry is to be paralyzed by recurrent revolts on the part of outraged human nature, it must satisfy criteria which are not purely economic.

A most elegant treatment of an ageless truth. Reality has a way of being "re-discovered," as if new. A less graceful, but fully corroborative, finding was issued by the American Productivity and Quality Center in 1991 (*Los Angeles Times,* d 1991). The Center found that challenging work was ranked as the most important job motivating factor. Recognition (pride) for a job well done came in second. Pay? It ranked fourth.

People who go to work, all of them humans, have goals other than simply making money. Money does not buy self-respect. Neither does fear. Workers who are treated like biological machines, in any setting, are reduced to roles of mere survival in environments of stifling fear. Fear and quality are incompatible.

Fear is a sweeping ailment in our workplaces. It is not only a common tool of management, but it is often an affliction of management itself. You don't think about quality when you're afraid. There are too many examples of policy based on fear.

When was the last time you went into a gas station and encountered a sign that chided you to "pay before pumping"?

You are required to walk to some distant kiosk and slip your credit card through a slot simply because management is afraid that you will fill your tank and merrily charge off without paying. I'm sure such events take place, but management's policy response is not to trust anyone. To the consumer, the policy of assuming that all customers are criminals appears to be based quite simply on fear. I recently had the following conversation at a local pump house.

"Do 1 have to give you my card before I pump?"

"Yes."

"How do I know you won't steal it?"

"What?"

"If you can't trust me to pump my gas and then pay you, how can I trust you with my credit card while my back is turned over there?"

"What?"

"Why are you so afraid of me?"

"What?"

These days I go further down the street to a station that has a sign "Please pump first." They're not afraid of me.

It touches all of us. My wife, Pat, recently bought me a very nice watch. She shopped around for it. At one store she noticed that the clerk would never place more than two watches on the counter at a time. Wanting to compare at least three at a reasonable visual range, she asked, "Could I see these three next to each other?"

"I'm only supposed to put two out at a time."

"Why?"

"It's a rule."

Pat had run into a management policy that assumed she would grab the third watch and run away with it—or some other concept motivated by fear. On the verge of spending more than a few dollars, she politely asked, "Would you mind if I spoke with the manager?"

Upon this inquiry, the clerk was visibly terrified. There was a problem and management was being called in. The conversation with the manager went as follows.

"I was just wondering why I can't look at three watches at a time."

"Oh, that's just a rule we have."

Pat did not raise her voice, "Does it bother you at all that I'm going to go someplace else and buy a watch?"

"I'm sorry, but we have to follow rules."

She left the rule-bound robots, who's fearful agenda excluded any considerations of customer service, to the next shoppers. No one can blame them. Management's policy of control through fear had touched them all: the clerk, visibly afraid of failing her supervisor; the manager, clearly unable to bend his own management's rule. Pat eventually found a proprietor that was not afraid of her. He was very polite and helpful. Later, she told me, "I've got one for the book."

And on it goes. Target is a sizeable retail chain of discount department stores that recorded $9 billion in sales during its 1991 fiscal year. The *Los Angeles Times* reports that management employs what they call district investigators, whose job it is to aggressively search for internal losses (*Los Angeles Times,* c 1992). District investigators have a quota—they are expected to terminate one employee every 18 hours. They do their job well. They have been known to interrogate an employee over a 2-day period behind locked doors, with threats to call the police. At least four respondents were falsely accused. They sued and won a tidy sum. They also lost their jobs through terminations and forced resignations.

Target management has not exactly empowered their workers to join in quality-oriented teamwork. How can they when their policy is to "weed out," on a quota basis, the "criminals" they themselves have hired? It's tough for an employee to concentrate on pride of workmanship and

customer service surrounded by covert, quota-hungry investigators—much less gain self-respect. Target has a target—its own people!

Significantly, Target management is not alone in dehumanizing its workers. Most managers would be appalled by the Target story and would assure us that no such policy could ever be in effect on their watch. Realize, however, that the mentality is largely a matter of degree. There remains a pervasive attitude in management that the workers are somehow lesser beings. Our institutions and cultural lore have taught our managers that they are managers because they know more about what has to be done than the workers. "After all, if they know more than me, how come I'm managing them? I got here because I'm smarter." And, by extension, they are led to the conclusion they are superior beings. The "my children" attitude is subtle and pervasive.

Check out this memo distributed throughout a high-tech organization largely comprised of top-rate scientists and Ph.D.'s:

> The President has requested that all managers and supervisors be reminded that the consumption of alcohol at holiday events held at our facility is prohibited. Employees are also expected to adhere to reasonable standards of conduct at holiday events held off-site. Adherence to these standards will help ensure a safe and healthy holiday season for all.

This "Be Nice Children and Don't Fight When You Go Out" memo, I am told, was widely received with disgust by one and all of the "children." Said one employee, "I don't think I need him to tell me to be nice. I am thoroughly offended. Every one I know has been angry about this for over a week."

"Why don't you go tell him?" I said.

"Are you kidding? He's the boss."

There are a number of descriptors for this. One is "High-tech Anger." Another is "High-tech Fear."

Fear has the peculiar property of being bidirectional Not only do people fear bosses, but bosses who don't understand what quality is all about often fear their underlings, especially when the "child" does such a good job that the boss senses the horror of being eclipsed.

Thomas Pickering, past U.S. Ambassador to the United Nations, found out that thinking swiftly and negotiating effectively without waiting for the boss might not always be a good idea. Considerable controversy surrounded the reasoning behind his curt removal in April 1992. Skeptics say that Pickering's problem was simple. He was too good. Richard N. Gardner, a Columbia University Professor of International Law, not only ranked Pickering as superb, but in some ways better than Adlai Stevenson and Arthur Goldberg. But James Baker didn't. No matter how closely Pickering adhered to existing policies, observers perceived that the Secretary of State sensed a lack of control. To the non–quality-oriented manager, the difference between empowerment and loss of control gets very confusing. When the difference is misunderstood, it also gets scary.

When asked at a Senate subcommittee hearing why he was transferring the ambassador to India, Baker replied (*Los Angeles Times,* e 1992), "Because the President instituted a policy of three years of service for both Foreign Service and career diplomats."

Dale Bumpers, Senator from Arkansas, didn't quite understand why the clock took precedence over performance. "So Tom's three years is up?" he asked incredulously.

"Yes, sir," answered Baker, "absolutely, and for no other reason."

Nobody said anything about quality or the terror experienced when one equates the responsibility of leadership with

absolute control. Noted one senior French diplomat on the scene: "It's pretty thin, isn't it?"

At his departing luncheon, Henry Kissinger introduced Pickering as: "Our distinguished ambassador...," and, after pausing for effect, added, "too distinguished for some people."

Quality in government, like anywhere else, must come from the very top. In the meantime, politicians remain especially good at underestimating "their children." During the heavy rains that came to Southern California in the winter of 1992, the water rose in the Sepulveda Flood Control Area at a startling rate—at times, over a foot per minute. People were caught in the area, and theatrical helicopter rescues were taking place. The golf course and surrounding roads were submerged. Treetops alone poked above the angry cascade. Radio and TV coverage was immediate, dramatic, live, and intense. Commuters got the latest news in a timely manner, and everyone with any sense avoided the area, even the "lookey-loo's." Who would go near it? Hours later, the situation was still wicked when the Governor interrupted useful news coverage to convey an idea he had. The thought went something like this: "... I urge all of you in the Los Angeles area to avoid the Sepulveda vicinity..."

This was a devastating blow to a bunch of us kids who were about to go down and attempt to tee off on the back nine. I sent a wire to the Governor, thanking him.

The children come in all sizes, colors, and sexes. Kathrine G. Thompson is a highly successful builder in Orange County, California. She is also very active in fund raising for charitable organizations as well as the Republican Party. As a member of "Team 100," one of a group of individuals who have contributed $100,000 or more, she was recently invited to a special reception with Clayton Yeutter, Chairman of the Republican National Committee. During the reception, Mr. Yeutter walked up to Ms. Thompson and said (*Los Angeles Times,* f 1992), "And who do you belong to, little lady?"

I wasn't there that evening, but I expect Ms. Thompson allowed him to know.

The antithesis of the "my children" mentality is found at Federal Express, where management has actively trained and encouraged their drivers to carry the ball for the company. The management at FE realizes that the main exposure of their organization to the public is via the employees that touch the public—not the managers in offices. The front-line cadre is encouraged to take any action they wish to ensure that customers are satisfied. The drivers aren't afraid of anybody at work. The FE attitude that "our fate is riding with you" has established a happy crew with a sense of value and self-respect. The policy, management believes, is directly attributable to their enviable position in the market. Check it out the next time FE knocks on your door. They're nice people. They work for a quality company.

The Quill Corporation of Lincolnshire, Illinois, is owned by the Miller family—Arnold, Harvey, and Jack. They sell office supplies to thousands of companies through mail and telephone orders. When the big office supply chains put the heat on, Quill dropped their prices, but all that did was cut into profits. What did Quill management do? The first thing they did was to forgo their own bonuses. Then they turned to the people with a bosom knowledge of process within the company—the employees. Once they were informed of the situation and asked to help, the workers came up with 1991 savings that boosted profits by 47 percent. Says Jack Miller (*Los Angeles Times,* g 1992): "We are a much better company now than we were before 1990. The management sets the major goals, but the people really doing the work are below the management level. They are meeting, using their brains and coming up with tremendous solutions. There are hundreds of ways to save without massive layoffs or sacrificing customer service. In fact, we are actually enhancing the level of customer service."

Quill is not a small company. They do $300 million per year. But any sized company can learn from them. You don't have to be big to figure it out.

The small business winner of the Baldrige Award in 1990 was Wallace Company, Inc. They make pipes, valves, and fittings. Chief executive W. Wallace is another good manager with the right attitude. He understands the relationship between shooting messengers and fear. Wallace is a listener and, when he hears a good suggestion from any source, he does something about it. Because Wallace sets the tone, everyone else in the organization is not afraid to do the same.

Brian Rowe, Senior Vice-President of General Electric's Aircraft Engine Company, is also a good manager. The first of the Fourteen Points that Rowe picked to implement was to drive out fear.

These gentlemen understand that you can't have dignity and fear at the same time. More simply, they know that, when messengers get shot, they either shut up or come up with numbers that management wants to hear. The epidemic is pervasive.

Deming (who else?) has a host of examples. One such case involved the monitoring of a stamping process through Statistical Process Control. Deming, through his intimate knowledge of the process involved, was able to quickly determine that the data were faulty. What was the problem? The problem was fear. Quite simply, the inspector was insecure. The story was that the manager would close the plant down if defective units reached 10 percent on any given day. The inspector has his loyalty, but it wasn't to quality. It was directed toward keeping the jobs of the 300 people around him—and his own.

"Don't make waves" is everywhere. Dr. Donald Berwick writes about the inspection dilemma that permeates the medical industry. The myriad of reports are highly suspect, if not useless. Says Berwick (Berwick 1989, 53):

The inspector says, "I will find you out if you are deficient." The subject replies, "I will therefore prove I am not deficient" and will seek not understanding, but escape. The signs of this game are everywhere in health care.

There's nothing easy about removing fear, even when quality programs are in place. SPC charts themselves don't solve problems if workers who uncover high levels of deviations feel that they will be blamed. Discussing problems openly takes trust. It doesn't happen when workers don't trust managers, managers don't trust workers, or managers don't trust managers.

Lack of trust is not new. It's only been around 100,000 years or so. In the *Republic,* Plato speaks of Socrates and *thymos.*

Thymos has to do with the soul, spirit, mind, and temper. It is akin to a sense of *justice* and *self-worth.* People innately believe they have a certain worth, and, when treated as though they are *worthless,* they become *angry.* The English word "indignation" is synonymous with the word anger. *Dignity* has to do with a people's sense of their own value and self-worth. Indignation arises when that sense of *worth* is carelessly affronted by others. Conversely, when other people sense that we are not behaving in accordance with our own sense of self-worth and *self-esteem,* we experience *shame.* But when we are judged in a manner that is consistent with our sense of self-worth, we experience *pride.*

An old and simple message. Most good ideas are simple. Yet it contains some of the most important words in our lives. Francis Fukuyama doesn't take them lightly. He contends that they are the expressions that drive all of humanity—and consequently all of history itself (Fukuyama 1992, 165).

Notice the absence of the words "power" and "money." Power and money may be mistaken as a means to *thymos,* but they are not what *thymos* is all about. Such words need to be remembered when we think about workers: justice, worth-less, worth, angry, indignation, dignity, self-worth, self-esteem, shame, and pride.

Any manager worth his NaCl should copy the message down and hang it in the office.

TRAINING

When workers don't trust managers, managers don't trust workers, and managers don't trust managers, there is a problem within the organization. The problem is training.

The first part of the problem is getting management to think differently—very differently. The change involves more than a revision or a transformation of existing structures. It requires a complete paradigm shift—a totally new structure.

There is negligible dispute among the gurus of quality that successful quality movements require more than simple commitment; it requires authentic passion on the part of top managers. Extensive training is essential to conducting any serious quality program. But, of course, nothing can begin until our "leaders" learn that *they* are among the assembly that has to be retrained That's why all training has to take place from the top down.

If leaders and their managers don't get it, nobody else can get it. And there's plenty of evidence to support that they still ain't got it. An uncomfortably sizable number of our managers and politicians are unwittingly sticking to the old ways as we near a new century. Most of them simply don't know what to do. And time is running out.

Recognition comes first, soberly and often painfully attained. Then comes the passion—an unusual kind of passion that must be at once sustained and tempered by patience. One of the reasons that quality movements require patience is because they require a great deal of training and retraining. Training takes time.

Before the passion for quality hits, managers often ask the same questions: "What's going to happen to productivity if we take time out to train thousands of employees? How long is all that going to take, and how much is all that going to cost?"

Motorola's adventure with quality is perhaps one of the more impressive in the country. Not the least reason for their success is the faith that Robert Galvin, Chairman of the Executive Committee, has that the benefits of training far outweigh the costs.

In Japan, the concept is a given. The Japanese don't think about the cost of quality, much less the cost of training. It is a natural part of the program. New employees typically begin their careers with 1 to 3 full years of schooling, depending on their technical training. They are educated with a mind-set toward quality and are given a thorough foundation in the tools required, including statistical process control. The Japan Productivity Center also agrees that well-educated employees are a must for any quality program.

The lesson learned by more and more organizations embarking on quality programs is that training and retraining must be taken seriously. Invariably, as programs mature, the awareness of management is heightened to this absolute necessity. Organizations that get obsessed with quality also get obsessed with training—no matter what the cost.

Just outside of Stuttgart, the Trumpf Company, maker of machine tools and flat metal parts, trains apprentices for 3½ years on the theory and practice of handling metals. For the first 6 months, students file pieces of metal in vises. That's all they do. After a while, they really begin to understand metal.

The Trumpf machines are computer controlled, but the machines are built and run by people. The Trumpf management believes that you must be able to work with your hands to really understand what a programmable machine is doing with a piece of metal. Trumpf employees do, and the quality shows. The philosophy is also contained in management's observation that the social status of manual work in the United States is low. It is the German view that everybody in the United States can do something, but nobody really understands or holds esteem for manual work. A misunderstanding largely due to our culture, with resounding impacts on quality.

But the training associated with quality goes beyond just picking up where our schools are deficient. Upper and middle managers must be trained to listen to workers. They must learn to take advantage of positive ideas and suggestions and to include the worker as an integral part of the quality effort, by allowing the worker to take on more responsibility.

The successful training effort must start at the top and then work down, level by level. It is of scant value to train personnel whose management does not understand the radical views that they will bring back from class. Training must take place at all levels, with emphasis toward middle management. By far, the highest threat of the quality movement is perceived at the middle management level. Workers tend to understand the required changes with more ease because they are at last being listened to and treated with new-found respect. Middle managers must undergo a complete flip in transforming themselves from "know-it-alls" to listeners—from bosses to leaders. It is a scary thing to grasp, and accomplishing it takes constant encouragement and reinforcement through education and training.

This point needs to be emphasized, underscored, stressed, and highlighted. It should also be accentuated. Be prepared to train middle managers, to watch and encourage them, and to train them again. Many of them will feel so threatened (crushed is a better word) that they will provide plenty of lip service but still be incapable of altering their historic life-styles and accompanying attitudes.

How about this conversation that recently took place at a QC circle team meeting between a manager and a worker at a leading high-tech aerospace organization? The worker was reporting on the team's recommendations, and his line manager was in the audience. *The line manager had been "trained" in TQM.*

WORKER: *"After my presentation, I'd like to go around the room and get an assessment from each of you on our team recommendations."*

MANAGER: *"We're not going to do that."*

WORKER: *"But I'd like to hear a free and honest assessment from everyone while the material is fresh."*

MANAGER: *We'll review your recommendations after the meeting."*

WORKER: *"But that's not my understanding of what TQM is."*

MANAGER: *"Don't worry about that. We're committed to TQM. Anyone around here who's not committed to TQM has a future that's in jeopardy."*

The manager had been trained, but he didn't get it. Not enough Thymos. He is in acute need of additional training.

Be prepared to retrain. If they don't get it, be prepared to let 'em go. There is nothing easy about this kind of training. It takes some corporate tough love. Nor are quality training programs simply added to existing internal educational structures and services. The Motorola experience is fundamental. They opened their own university that services their locations worldwide. A minimum of 1 week of training is required of every employee each year. Motorola thinks nothing of spending millions on training, year in and year out.

Again, you don't have to be big. When quality hits, so does training. It has to. The much smaller Wallace Company, with 280 employees, has spent $2 million on formal quality program training.

Ernie Schaefer was once described by GM management as "somewhat of a revolutionary . . . the perfect guy for the job because he believed in the quality of his people." He came to the Chevrolet Van Nuys, California plant in 1984. Schaefer was, of course, more than conversant in the quality team concept. He was one of the old Fiero bunch. In order to turn Van Nuys into a team, Schaefer set up a training program with a $20 million grant from the State of California. Everyone in the plant, managers and workers alike, went through a week of team training on an array of subjects, from safety and financial systems to ergonomics and conflict resolution. Leaders of teams got an additional five weeks of training. Even before the team concept began to be implemented, enough good will was generated to improve the plant's performance. Van Nuys, for years at the bottom of GM's quality audits, shot up to the number-three ranking for a time. Repairs dropped nearly 15 percent. (Gabor, Seamonds 1987)

It is clear that there can be no success in any quality movement without extensive, sensitive, and, yes, painful training. Once top management has crossed the threshold, the biggest obstacle to company acceptance will be in middle management and in lower-line management. The training must take place from the top down. Middle management must be treated with patience, positive compassion, and dignity. After the boss, *they* have the toughest transition to make.

Here's a good tough love course opener for middle management:

The middle management loyalty vector in the United States is always pointing upward. It is positioned by ego and fear. If U.S. managers truly wish to attain quality, they must abandon their egos and fear and begin directing their loyalty vectors downward. That's where the knowledge is. This lesson is 90 percent of your training.

PART 4

IMPLEMENTATION
GUIDELINES

■ For organizations starting out cold, outside help is invariably required and wisely sought. The experience pool is growing. Typical starting points include attendance at seminars, the direct retainer of gurus or consultants who know what they're doing, and benchmark visits to organizations that have had successful (and not so successful) experiences.

The ranks of organizations *talking* quality are growing every nanosecond. Assume for a moment that you are chosen to be the new "quality" coordinator at your organization. Here are some guidelines, harvested from the schooled, to consider before you take it on.

WHERE IS MANAGEMENT?

Don't even try it unless your very top manager has a complete preoccupation with quality—an absolute fetish. Your top manager must find it impossible to learn of anything that is less than perfect without wanting to fix it immediately. Absolutely immediately!

"Fixing it immediately" does not mean conducting extensive analysis devoted to possible legal, technical, advertising, sales, union, cost, schedule, recall, or other programmatic impacts and least of all coming up with a damage control plan. "Fixing it" means stopping everything now, going directly to where it happened, finding out exactly what happened, and correcting it. Period. If you have any doubts about this, give your top manager four or five books to read and ask for a meeting in 2 weeks. If you are considered to be "uppity," then stuff the whole thing. Get another assignment, or maybe another job! Quality isn't going to happen.

If your meeting with the top manager comes off, it need only be a short one. Ask if a genuine seizure of obsession has taken place. Ask if personal behavior patterns are actually changing. Ask if quality has become a voracious passion. Find out if there is a new-found gut hunger, not of the belly kind so easily banished by protein, but the kind expressed by Apple's Debi Coleman (Peters 1988, 71):

> "I don't think you should ever manage anything that you don't care passionately about."

If the answer to all four questions is: Yes! Yes! Yes! Yes!—then take the assignment. If you don't get all four, don't touch it!

MAKE A PLAN

Whether you tailor your plan on Deming, Feigenbaum, Juran, Ishikawa, Crosby, another organization, or someone else is not critical. What is critical is to make one and execute it. Modifications will invariably be called for to guide the plan toward success in your own organization. But they should only be that—modifications.

There is a generic four-step sequence to a successful plan. The sequence is: train, define initial application(s), execute initial application, and expand applications. Carry out each of these steps using the Plan-Do-Check-Act (PDCA) cycle.

TRAINING

Always start your training at the top. Initial training must be directed at the top boss and the cadre of top management (vice-presidents, executive directors, deputy directors, assistant directors, division managers, etc.). Why will the cadre all come and listen intently? Because the boss started the whole thing, personally "invited" them, and is in attendance. They have been conditioned to do that. Their upwardly turned vector of loyalty works to the advantage of quality's beginnings. They are about to be retrained. When they become converts, they in turn will personally invite the next level down, and so forth. Their loyalty vector will begin to point downward.

Start by covering the Fourteen Points. Use plenty of examples, covering the entire spectrum of modern quality concepts. Supplement instruction with professional quality trainers and experienced, outside speakers to reinforce material. Give your students every book you can find on the subject. Give them specific assignments related to the implementation of quality programs. Examples of topics for assignments: the use of quality circles, definition of customers, the training of middle managers, supplier practices, use of Statistical Process Control, the cost of quality, the dimensions of fear in the workplace, traditional management attitudes, departmental barriers, policies on quotas and slogans, leadership vs. bossing in the quality setting, the virtues of empowerment, annual review practices, simple humanity, and so on. Send them to seminars and to other organizations to research their assignments, and have them present their findings to the class. Hang the cost.

Carry out PDCA in this initial top management training effort. Have the class participate in PDCA cycles. When you're satisfied that top management has embraced the cause, you are ready to define an initial application. At the same time, continue training in parallel by moving on to the training of middle management using the same processes. Then, on to the workers!

DEFINE AN INITIAL APPLICATION

While your training program continues through the ranks, use your newly trained upper management team to select an initial application area. Give them assignments to verify their ideas, with initial data gathered from the actual workplace. Have them personally collect the data. Don't let them delegate it! Eventually, you will want the ideas to originate from lower levels, but you are just now beginning and you need the excitement and involvement of top management. Screen all ideas with your students for one that has the best probability for success. That is, pick a problem area that you all agree can be improved in a reasonable period of time. The application should cross functional boundaries within your organization. You're not ready for outside customers and suppliers yet. You need more experience.

Select your first vertically and horizontally integrated QC circle team to work the problem. The team should consist of actual workers, with an intimate knowledge of the process under study, and their managers. But keep the team small—less than ten people. Concentrate on team members that *really* understand the work environment. If you have to, go thin on managers. But be sure that management has first been properly trained. If the managers have been properly trained, they know they don't really need to be there. They will empower the workers who have the answers. There needs to be a complete vertical understanding of what you're doing. While training may not be a sufficient condition for success, it is definitely a necessary condition.

Bring your first team in and put them through the training course. Concentrate on PDCA. By now you have a better training program than the one you started out with, and you will continue to improve it with this new experience.

Don't cut the new QC circle team loose until you are convinced that everyone on the new team has undergone a complete attitude adjustment and is passionate about trying out what they have learned.

EXECUTE THE APPLICATION

Empower the team to act on their own, no matter what the consequences. Stay with them, acting as the first facilitator in your organization. Guide them through the PDCA cycles. Document the process through meeting minutes and your own notes.

If the team fails to find better process in their problem area, do the cycle again. You must be passionate about succeeding the first time out. If you have made a bad choice of the first problem and if you collectively become convinced that no improvement is possible, find and admit your mistake. Drop the assignment, go back to the management team, get a new problem, and form a new QC circle team. Analyze your PDCA cycle and learn from it. You cannot possibly quit because you believe. Your mix of zeal and patience is too immortal.

When the first team succeeds, identify a new problem. Make up a second team and do it all over again. Get two or three successes under your belt. As each improvement is realized, wrap up your documentation and disband the team. Do not create permanent mini-bureaucracies. Remember turf!

EXPAND APPLICATIONS

Pick one or more applications based on your growing experience. The original management team is a source of further applications. By now, however, your parallel training program has created an expanded resource base. Look for application ideas close to the bottom of the vertical structure. Ask the workers for ideas. Managers don't really know much about the specifics of improving quality. They are too far from the real work. Workers know more about their jobs than anybody. All you have to do is include them by asking.

As you build more teams, monitor their progress carefully. Take every opportunity you can to dispense honest compliments. Expand in a cautious and success-oriented fashion. Constantly identify candidates to act as additional trainers and as facilitators on future teams.

When you believe you have a feel for the process, begin to expand cross-functionally beyond the organization to the total system by including suppliers and external customers. Build special training courses tailored just for them. Get them actively on your team. Identify and include the entire system, all the way upstream and downstream.

FINALLY

Be prepared to spend 3 to 5 years before the culture is changed and success is achieved. Remember, you are in a process that:

1. Is difficult to start; and

2. Never really ends.

Throughout it all, you must be critical, direct, sensitive, leathery, forbearing, aggressive, empathetic, single minded, community minded, ever positive, devoid of fear, and very, very patient.

Philip Crosby counsels us that the hardest lesson for the implementor of quality to learn is that authentic improvement just plain takes time to realize (Crosby 1980, 108).

Your *single,* most *powerful* tool is the latent need in everyone for individual worth, pride, responsibility, and dignity in the workplace. That powerful tool silently waits there for you. Take it up! Use it! The focus is the common passion for quality. Quality above all else!

The achievement of system-wide quality is at once difficult and incredibly easy. No one is going away. We are all together. To find our own potential, we must find everyone's potential. To realize our own dreams, we must realize everyone's dreams. When everyone's vision is to achieve quality, when all else becomes subordinate, when humans become humane in that pursuit—that's when "Quality" happens.

APPENDIX A TRADE AND PROFESSIONAL ASSOCIATIONS

American Astronautical Society
c/o Dr. Peter B. Boyce
1630 Connecticut Ave., NW, Suite 200
Washington, DC 20009
(202) 328-2010

American Automatic Control Council
c/o EECS
Northwestern University
2145 Sheridan Rd.
Evanston, IL 60208-3118
(708) 491-3641

**American Institute of Aeronautics and Astronautics—
Technical Information Division**
555 W. 57th St., Suite 1200
New York, NY 10019
(212) 247-6500

American Productivity and Quality Center
123 N. Post Oak Lane, Suite 300
Houston, TX 77024-7797
(713) 681-4020

American Productivity Management Association
300 N. Martingale Rd., Suite 230
Schamburg, IL 60173
(708) 619-2909

American Society for Engineering Management
P.O. Box 867
Annapolis, MD 21401
(410) 263-7065

American Society for Quality Control
611 E. Wisconsin Ave.
Milwaukee, Wisconsin 53202
(414) 272-8575

American Supplier Institute
15041 Commerce Dr., South
Dearborn, MI 48120-1238
(313) 336-8877

Association of Computer Professionals
9 Forest Dr.
Plainview, NY 11803
(516) 938-8223

Automobile Manufacturers Association
1620 Eye St., NW
Washington, DC 20006
(202) 775-2716

Engineering Society of Detroit
100 Farnsworth Ave.
Detroit, MI 48202
(313) 832-5400

European Organization for Quality
P.O. Box 5032 CH-3001
Berne, Switzerland

IEEE Engineering Management Society
c/o Institute of Electrical and Electronic Engineers
345 E. 47th St.
New York, NY 10017
(212) 705-7900

Institute for the Advancement of Engineering
24300 Calvert St.
Woodland Hills, CA 91367-1113
(818) 992-8292

Institute of Environmental Sciences
940 E. Northwest Hwy.
Mt. Prospect, IL 60056
(708) 255-1561

Japan Productivity Center
National Engineering Consortium
303 E. Wacker Dr., Suite 740
Chicago, IL 60601
(312) 938-3500

National Institute of Standards and Technology (NIST)
Gaithersburg, MD 20899
(301) 975-2000

Product Development and Management Association
c/o Thomas P. Hustad
Indiana University
Graduate School of Business
801 W. Michigan Ave.
Indianapolis, IN 46202-5151
(800) 232-5241

Society of Automotive Engineers
400 Commonwealth Dr.
Warrendale, PA 15096-0001
(412) 776-4841

Society of Manufacturing Engineers
P.O. Box 930
1 SME Dr.
Dearborn, MI 48121
(313) 271-1500

APPENDIX B QUALITY-RELATED ACADEMIC PROGRAMS

■ This appendix lists quality-related academic programs offered at colleges and universities throughout the country and indicates their offerings at the graduate, bachelor, associate, certificate, and continuing education levels.

As with all listings related to quality, the number of programs is expanding constantly, most notably at state university and state college systems. Check with your local schools and colleges first.

Institution	Programs Offered (see key below)
Arizona State University Tempe, AZ	G, B
Arkansas State University Beebe, AR	A, C, CE
Baylor University Waco, TX	G, B
Brigham Young University Provo, UT	G, B
California State University Chico, CA Dominguez Hills, CA Long Beach, CA Northridge, CA	G, B, CE G B CE
Columbia State Community College Columbia, TN	A, CE
Community College of S. Nevada Las Vegas, NV	A
Cowley County Community College Arkansas City, KS	A, C, CE
DeAnza College Cupertino, CA	A, CE
Eastern Kentucky University Richmond, KY	A
Eastern Michigan University Ypsilanti, MI	G, B, CE
Elizabethtown Community College Elizabethtown, KY	A, CE

Program Key: G = Graduate, B = Bachelor, A = Associate,
C = Certificate, CE = Continuing Education.

Institution	Programs Offered (see key below)
Forsyth Technical Community College Winston-Salem, NC	A, CE
George Washington University Washington, DC	G, B, C, CE
Georgia State University Atlanta, GA	B
Grove City College Grove City, PA	B
Harvard Business School Boston, MA	G
Indiana Vocational Training College Terre Haute, IN	A, C, CE
Iowa State University Ames, IA	G, B, CE
Jacksonville State University Jacksonville, AL	B, C, CE
Kansas Newman College Wichita, KS	B, A
Langston University Langston, OK	B, A
Lansing Community College Lansing, MI	A, CE
LeTourneau University Longview, TX	B
Lorain County Community College Elyria, OH	A, C, CE

Program Key: G = Graduate, B = Bachelor, A = Associate, C = Certificate, CE = Continuing Education.

Institution	Programs Offered (see key below)
Marion College of Fond du Lac Fond du Lac, WI	G, B
Mohave Community College Kingman, AZ	G, B, A, C, CE
North Carolina A&T University Greensboro, NC	G, B, C
Northwestern University Evanston, IL	G, B
Ohio State University Columbus, OH	G
Owens Technical College Toledo, OH	A, CE
Pennsylvania State University University Park, PA	G, B, CE
Polytechnic University Farmingdale, NY	G, CE
Purdue University West Lafayette, IN	G, B, C, CE
Roane State Community College Harriman, TN	A, C, CE
Rochester Institute of Technology Rochester, NY	G, B
Rutgers University Pisctaway, NJ	G, B, CE
San Jose State University San Jose, CA	G, B

Program Key: G = Graduate, B = Bachelor, A = Associate,
C = Certificate, CE = Continuing Education.

Institution	Programs Offered (see key below)
Southeast Community College Lincoln, NE	A, CE
Southern College of Technology Marietta, GA	G, B, CE
St. Louis Community College St. Louis, MO	A, CE
State University College–Buffalo Buffalo, NY	B
State University of New York–Buffalo Buffalo, NY	G, B
Texas A&M University College Station, TX	G, B, CE
Tri-County Technical College Pendleton, SC	A, C, CE
Union College Schenectady, NY	G
University of Alabama Tuscaloosa, AL	G, B
University of Alaska–Fairbanks Fairbanks, AL	G
University of Arizona Tuscon, AZ	G
University of Arkansas Fayetteville, AR	G, B
University of California Santa Barbara, CA	CE

Program Key: G = Graduate, B = Bachelor, A = Associate,
C = Certificate, CE = Continuing Education.

Institution	Programs Offered (see key below)
University of Central Florida Orlando, FL	G, B
University of Dayton Dayton, OH	G, B, CE
University of Idaho Moscow, ID Idaho Falls, ID	G, B, CE B
University of Iowa Iowa City, IA	G, B
University of Maryland College Park, MD	CE
University of Massachusetts Amherst, MA	G
University of Miami Coral Gables, FL	G, B, A, CE
University of Minnesota–Twin Cities Minneapolis, MN	G, B, C, CE
University of New Mexico Albuquerque, NM	G, B, CE
University of South Carolina Columbia, SC	G, B, CE
University of Southern California Los Angeles, CA	C, CE
University of Indiana Evansville, IN	G, B, CE
University of Southern Maine Gorham, ME	B

Program Key: G = Graduate, B = Bachelor, A = Associate,
C = Certificate, CE = Continuing Education.

Institution	Programs Offered (see key below)
University of Tampa Tampa, FL	G
University of Tennessee Knoxville, TN	CE
University of Vermont Burlington, VT	G, B, CE
University of Wisconsin Madison, WI Menomonie, WI	G, B, CE G, B
Washington Institute of Technolgy Vienna, VA	CE
West Virginia University Morgantown, WV	G, B
Wichita State University Wichita, KS	G, B, CE
Xavier University Cincinnati, OH	G

Program Key: G = Graduate, B = Bachelor, A = Associate,
C = Certificate, CE = Continuing Education.

APPENDIX C INTERNATIONAL, NATIONAL, AND STATE AWARDS

■ Quality awards are proliferating around the world. To date, some 33 countries are offering awards related to some aspect of the quality movement—an increase of almost 50 percent in the last three years. Many organizations report that the application and competition for an award is well worth the effort, since the process invariably leads to a strenuous examination of internal strengths and weaknesses.

This appendix lists awards for which any company in the world is eligible, national awards presented within the United States, and state-sponsored awards for which organizations operating totally or partially within states are eligible. New offers appear at every level almost monthly.

INTERNATIONAL QUALITY AWARDS FOR WHICH U.S. ORGANIZATIONS ARE ELIGIBLE

The Deming Prize
The Union of Japanese Scientists and Engineers
Tokyo, Japan
Recipients: Individuals, companies, factories, divisions

European Quality Award
The European Foundation for Quality Management
Eindhoven, The Netherlands
Recipients: Companies

International Academy for Quality Award
International Academy for Quality
Hampton, United Kingdom
Recipients: Individuals, for a technical paper, management paper, or individual achievement

Internatonal Benchmarking Awards
International Benchmarking Clearinghouse
Houston, TX
Recipients: Companies

Award of Professional Excellence
The Society for Human Resource Management
Alexandria, VA
Recipients: Individuals

U.S. QUALITY AWARDS

Award of Professional Excellence
The Society for Human Resource Management
Alexandria, VA
Recipients: Individuals

Malcomb Baldrige National Quality Award
National Institute of Standards and Technology
Gaithersburg, MD
Recipients: American companies

George M. Low Trophy
NASA Quality & Productivity Improvement Programs and The
  American Society for Quality Control
Milwaukee, WI
Recipients: Members of NASA's contractor community

Presidential Award for Duality
The Federal Quality Institute
Washington, DC
Recipients: Federal organizations

The Quality Improvement Prototype Award
The Federal Quality Institute
Washington, DC
Recipients: Federal organizations

The New England Quality Institute Leadership Award
The New England Quality Institute
Boston, MA
Recipients: Individuals

The Shingo Prize for Excellence in Manufacturing
Utah State University
Logan, UT
Recipients: American companies

Pennsylvania Quality Award
AMP Incorporated
Harrisburg, PA
Recipients: (to be established in 1994)

Tennessee Quality Award
National Center for Quality
Blountville, TN
Recipients: Public and private sector organizations

Texas Quality Award
American Productivity & Quality Center
Houston, TX
Recipients: Organizations

U.S. Senate Productivity Award for Virginia and Award for Continuing Excellence
Virginia Productivity Center & the SPA Board
Blacksburg, VA
Recipients: Public and private sector organizations

Wyoming Governor's Duality Award
Wyoming Dept. of Commerce
Cheyenne, WY
Recipients: Businesses

GLOSSARY

ANSI/ASQC Standards   American National Standards Institute/American Society for Quality Control standards; equivalent to ISO 9000 standards.

Barrier   A manifestation of aging businesses characterized by the construction of barricades around departments, the duplication of charters within sand boxes, and the inability to accept anything invented elsewhere (also known symptomatically as NIH—not invented here).

Boss   An individual who's fear, uncertainty, and lack of knowledge and training is exemplified by the issuing of unresearched, unilateral orders (See **Leader.**)

Benchmarking   An organized process of comparing one organization's performance in a given area with another organization in an effort to improve quality.

Common cause in variation   A source of unacceptable variation in a process due to the inherent operation of a system. Common causes can only be eliminated by management's action to improve a system design. It is estimated that 95 percent of control limit deviations are attributable to common causes. (See **Special cause in variation.**)

Composite organization   An arrangement of self-managing teams in a workplace empowered to meet management goals through their own initiatives. (See **Conventional organization.**)

Concurrent engineering   A systematic approach to creating a product that integrates all elements of the product life cycle from conception to disposal. The simultaneous consideration of product design, manufacturing, and logistics support design. In the quality lore, concurrent engineering emphasizes the complete upstream and downstream collaboration of customers, suppliers, marketing, finance, engineering, manufacturing, sales, customer support, and anyone else in the system.

Control chart   Any of a number of charts designed to statistically track variation of a process against upper and lower limits.

Control limits   Measurable upper and lower limits against which the statistical variability of a process is compared to assist in identifying special and common causes of variation.

Conventional organization   An organization in which work is organized hierarchically into separate functions and responsibility is deployed hierarchically. An inherent assumption in the conventional organization is that individuals further up the chain are more knowledgeable about all aspects of the workplace than those further down the chain.

CWQC   Company Wide Quality Control is a term commonly used in Japan.

Customer   An organization, department, or individual that receives goods and/or services from another organization, department, or individual. Examples are: a) supplier organizations providing materials to manufacturing organizations, b) a manufacturing department receiving designs from an engineering department, and c) the end user of a product.

Deming Prize   The most prominent international quality award, established in 1951 by the Union of Japanese Scientists and Engineers. The award is given annually in November to companies, company divisions, small companies, and factories for excellence in the use of statistical methods for CWQC.

Design for manufacturability   A product of concurrent engineering designed to improve the quality of a product by improving efficiency, reducing costs, and reducing variation in manufacturing. The concept is also applicable to design for test, design for operations, so on.

Employee participation circles   See **Quality Control circle.**

Empowerment   The distribution of power to lower-level personnel in an organization for the detailed implementation of quality based on management guidelines. A concept feared by conventional bosses and used to great advantage by leaders.

Facilitator   An expert in the training of personnel in subjects and processes related to quality. One who assists in guiding the work of a Quality Control circle or equivalent team.

Fear   A prevalent and accepted condition, never openly discussed, under which American managers, middle managers, and workers suffer. A tool in the arsenal of a boss. A condition eliminated by leaders.

Fourteen Points A set of tenets advanced by W. Edwards Deming for the achievement of quality.

Harvesting Refers to the traditional act of culling out unacceptable products following manufacture in an effort to achieve quality after the fact.

Hoshin Planning A methodology in which middle managers select key activities for improvement that are derived from top level management policies and develop quantitative goals for their realization.

Inspection A traditional term associated with quality assurance carried out in the act of harvesting. Constant reduction in the need for inspection is a common fallout of the constant enhancement of total system quality.

ISO 9000 A set of five quality management standards developed in 1987 for service and manufacturing industries by the International Organization for Standards.

Kaizen A process-oriented Japanese concept of gradual and unending improvement, as opposed to traditional Western short-term result-oriented concepts.

Leader An individual who exhibits a peculiar capacity to communicate specific goals at a level that can be understood by his or her subordinates and then delegates the accomplishment of those goals through training and empowerment without fear.

Malcomb Baldrige National Quality Award The most prominent quality award offered within the United

States, instituted by the National Institute of Standards and Technology.

Management by Objective   The practice of focusing on a narrow, simplistic organizational goal without regard to total system consequences. An example is, "Reduce costs by 30%." MOB can always be achieved at the expense of other desirable attributes, notably quality.

Middle managers   Classically, an unfortunate set of conventionally trained individuals caught between the old and the new. They typically, through no fault of their own, need more retraining than anyone else to accept the quality mind-set paradigm shift. They are, however, a set of individuals who have a significant leadership opportunity to translate top-level management goals through the implementation of quality-oriented tools and processes.

Plan-Do-Check-Act   A paradigm for the execution of activities of a Quality Control circle based on the Shewhart Cycle. The PDCA cycle consist of: a) problem definition and solution planning, b) execution of the change or test, c) measurement of the outcome, and d) implementation of a change or reversion to development of a better plan. The cycle is often repeated in a constant effort to improve quality.

Policy deployment   A quality-oriented, long-term planning mind-set developed at Bridgestone and Toyota, encompassing: a) top management's commitment to quality and willingness to listen, b) middle management's ability to coordinate goal-oriented teams, and c) freedom of the workers to develop problem solutions. Policy deployment focuses on the use of measurable, long-term planning strategies for continuous improvement and their layered integration throughout all levels of an organization.

Process A set of activities that describe a well-defined, end-to-end procedure.

Process control The act of measuring and regulating a process through the use of a quantitative method such as Statistical Process Control.

Quality A communicable obsession to constantly improve customer satisfaction.

Quality control The act of planning for, implementing, and managing quality. Traditional quality control relies heavily on reactive inspection. Modern quality control encompasses proactive control of total system processes.

Quality Control circle A representation of workers, supervisors, and middle managers across organizational boundaries to improve a process as it affects the improvement of quality. Organizations often establish their own unique terms for QC circles. Examples are employee participation teams, total quality teams, process action teams, so on.

Quality Function Deployment (QFD) A structured approach to determination of of system requirements. The starting point is the gathering of the customers' needs expressed in their own words. QFD proponents call this "the voice of the customer." The expressed needs are translated into technical "whats" and "hows" and are represented in a weighted matrix that facilitates design trade-off discussion and the making of design decisions. The goal is to insure that customer input is faithfully represented in final specifications. Extensions of the QFD concept can be carried out throughout the design process to assist in risk analysis, cost control, and so on.

Quota A form of Management By Objective where an assignment of production or service units to be fabricated by individuals is made on the assumption that they are all identical biological automata.

Ranking A process of employee evaluation in which half are ranked above average and half are ranked below average, independent of what they are doing. Ranking is widely used as a basis for justifying raises and determining advancements. In quality organizations, leaders naturally arise in a setting that allows all to reach their inherent potentials. Raises are based on achievement and experience. Thus, by definition, quality organizations don't have average people because they don't know who they are. *They don't define them.*

Responsibility A state assumed by an organization or individual at the behest of another in which the ability to act without guidance or superior authority is enabled. *Caution: Never accept responsibility without authority.*

Slogan A simplistic statement circulated by elitist management that believes the "people" are not capable of understanding the complex. Slogans are designed to instill incentive in workers who are deprived of motivation, responsibility, and authority by management.

Special cause in variation A source of unacceptable variation in a process due a temporary or transient condition. Special causes typically do not require significant system corrections or redesign (See **Common cause in variation.**)

Statistical process control A tool used for the statistical measurement of a process relative to upper and lower control limits, the identification of common and special causes of variation, and the development of strategies for the constant narrowing of control limits.

Supplier   An organization, department, or individual that provides goods and/or services to another organization, department, or individual.

System   In the engineering sense, an interdependent group of units (subsystems) that perform together as a functional whole. In his early quality work, Homer Sarasohn viewed any business or service organization as part of a "system." For Sarasohn, the system involves materials coming in, the organization itself, other organizations, and the means of getting outputs to end-user customers that make them happy.

Systems engineering   The systematic application of standards, procedures, and tools to the technical organization, management, and establishment of system requirements, design, fabrication, integration, testing, production, and logistics support.

System design team   An organization led by a systems engineer throughout the complete product development process. The system design team is the focal point for all system-related activities, including development of requirements, design, fabrication, integration, logistics support, manufacture, test, and product acceptance. The system design team establishes and coordinates Quality Control circles as required to improve systems engineering and related processes.

Taguchi Method   A team-oriented method for the planning, design, conducting, and analysis of experiments.

Thymos   A concept attributable to Socrates by Plato. It is analogous to an inner sense of justice and self-worth. A more generic motivator than power or money, thymos is an intrinsic condition that people experience in an organization that has successfully implemented a quality program.

Training   In the quality movement, training refers to educational programs designed to provide the complete quality-oriented mental paradigm shift and the technical tool set required by all personnel at all levels. Quality training programs should be distinct from existing instructional programs.

TQC   Total Quality Control is a term that was first introduced by Armand Feigenbaum in his book of the same title.

Voice of the customer   See **Quality Function Deployment.**

Worker   An individual who is in the most knowledgeable position to accomplish the goals of an organization and its leaders.

BIBLIOGRAPHY

Barlett, D., and J. Steele. 1992. *America: What Went Wrong?* Kansas City, MO.: Andrews & McMeel.

Berwick, Donald. 1989. Continuous improvement as an ideal in health care. *New England Journal of Medicine*, January 1989, 53.

Boardman, Thomas. 1992. The role of statistics and statisticians in total quality management. Paper presented at the Seventeenth Annual Summer Institute of Applied Statistics, Brigham Young University, June 1992.

Browne, Lewis. 1942. *Something Went Wrong.* New York: The MacMillan Company.

Charlotte Sun Herald. 1992. County to spend $117,000 for "quality management." 1 April 1992.

Crosby, Philip. 1980. *Quality Is Free.* New York: Penguin Books.

Deming, W. Edwards. 1982. *Out Of The Crisis.* Cambridge, Ma.: Massachusetts Institute of Technology Center for Advance Engineering Study.

Fabrycky, W., and B. Blanchard. 1990. *Systems Engineering and Analysis.* Englewood Cliffs, N.J.: Prentice Hall.

Fukuyama, Francis. 1992. *The End Of History And The Last Man.* New York: The Free Press, MacMillan, Inc.

Gabor, Andrea, and Jack A. Seamonds. 1987. GM's bootstrap battle: the factory-floor view. *U.S. News & World Report*, September 21, 1987, 52.

Gleick, James. 1987. *Chaos, Making A New Science.* New York: Penguin Books.

Howard, J. Daniel. 1993. Opening address, Western Regional Conference, American Society for Quality Control, Oxnard, California, February 1993.

Kuriloff, A. 1963. An experiment in management: putting theory Y to the test. *Personnel* (November–December): 8–17.

Los Angeles Times, a. Detroit's struggle to shift gears. 30 May 1992.

Los Angeles Times, b. Not your father's Democrats. 12 July 1992.

Los Angeles Times, c. TARGET: court upholds $5-million award to 4 ex-employees. 13 May 1992.

Los Angeles Times, d. Money won't buy love and at work won't buy happiness. 16 September 1991.

Los Angeles Times, e. Too good to last? 27 April 1992.

Los Angeles Times, f. Erase the "little lady" frame of mind. 2 February 1992.

Los Angeles Times, g. Workers find creative ways to cut costs. 21 February 1992.

Peters, Tom. 1988. *Thriving On Chaos.* New York: Alfred A. Knopf.

Reilly, Norman B. 1993. *Successful Systems Engineering For Engineers and Managers.* New York: Van Nostrand Reinhold.

Riley, R. M. Cadillac motor car's turnaround. Luncheon address presented at the Second International Symposium, National Council on Systems Engineering, Seattle, Washington, July 1992.

Scott, William. Military report. *Aviation Week and Space Technology,* 19 March 1990, 75.

Smith, Bruce. Competition and tighter budgets push aerospace firms toward TQM. *Aviation Week and Space Technology*, 9 December 1991, 56.

Star Free Press, a. Ventura, Ca. Quality awareness heightened in the U.S. 31 May 1992.

Star Free Press, b. Ventura, Ca. Bad Boss is not a laughing matter. 28 June 1992.

Trist, E., G. Higgin, H. Murray, and A. Pollock. 1963. *Organizational Choice*. London: Tavistock.

SUGGESTED FURTHER READING

■ There are thousands of introductory and advanced books related to quality on the market and more coming out every month. This appendix offers a shortened list designed to cover major topics and classic offerings as a starting point. It is far from exhaustive.

The books by Aguayo, Dobyns, Gabor, and Walton offer general and informative overviews of the quality movement in the United States. Imai's book offers a good perspective from Japan, and Ishikawa's book is a recognized classic. The remaining books in the introductory list are also excellent reading.

The advanced list includes books that offer in-depth coverage of topics such as quality function deployment, statistical quality control, effective utilization of teams, Taguchi methods, and benchmarking. *The ISO 9000 Handbook* is also included for those interested in the International Organization for Standardization's efforts to develop and promote worldwide quality standards.

These books are also valuable in providing extensive references for further reading.

BOOKS—INTRODUCTORY

Aguayo, Rafael. 1990. *Dr. Deming, The American Who Taught The Japanese About Quality.* New York: Carol Publishing Co.

Barlett, Donald, and James Steele. 1992. *America: What Went Wrong?* Kansas City: Andrews and McMeel.

Bracey, Hyler, J. Rosenblum, A. Sanford, and R. Trueblood. 1991. *Managing From the Heart.* New York: Delacorte Press.

Crosby, Philip. 1980. *Quality is Free.* New York: Penguin Books.

Dobyns, Lloyd, and Clare Crawford-Mason. 1991. *Quality Or Else.* Boston: Houghton Mifflin Company.

Gabor, Andrea. 1990. *The Man Who Discovered Quality.* New York: Times Books, Random House.

Imai, Masaaki. 1986. *Kaizen: The Key to Japan's Competitive Success.* New York: Random House.

Ishikawa, Kaoru. 1986. *Guide to Quality Control.* Tokyo: Union of Japanese Scientists and Engineers.

Osborne, David, and T. Gaebler. 1992. *Reinventing Government.* Reading, MA: Addison-Wesley.

Peters, Tom. 1988. *Thriving On Chaos.* New York: Alfred A. Knopf.

Walton, Mary. 1991. *Deming Management At Work.* New York: Perigree Books.

BOOKS—ADVANCED

Akao, Yoji. 1990. *Quality Function Deployment: Integrating Customer Requirements into Product Design*. Cambridge, MA: Productivity Press.

Deming, W. Edwards. 1986. *Out of the Crisis*. Cambridge, MA: Massachusetts Institute of Technology Center for Advanced Engineering Studies.

Grant, Eugene, and R. Leavenworth. 1988. *Statistical Quality Control, Sixth Edition*. New York: McGraw-Hill.

Huge, Ernest. 1990. *Total Quality: An Executive's Guide for the 1990's*. Homewood, IL: Business One Irwin.

Juran, Joseph. 1988. *Juran's Quality Control Handbook*. New York: McGraw-Hill.

Kinlaw, Dennis. 1992. *Continuous Improvement and Measurement for Total Quality: A Team-Based Approach*. San Diego: Pfeiffer & Company.

Lochner, Robert, and J. Matar. 1990. *Designing for Quality*. White Plains, NY: Quality Resources.

Peace, Glen Stuart. 1993. *Taguchi Methods: A Hands-on Approach*. Reading, PA: Addison Wesley.

Peach, Robert. 1992. *The ISO 9000 Handbook*. Fairfax, VA.: CEEM Information Services.

Ross, Phillip. 1988. *Taguchi Techniques for Quality Engineering*. New York: McGraw-Hill.

Shewhart, Walter. 1986. *A Statistical Method for the Viewpoint of Quality*. New York: Dover.

Scholtes, Peter. 1988. *The Team Handbook*. Madison, WI: Joiner Associates, Inc.

Spendolini, Michael. 1992. *The Benchmarking Book*. New York: AMACOM.

Wheeler, Donald. 1986. *Understanding Statistical Process Control, Second Edition*. Knoxville, TN: SPC Press.

Wellins, Richard, W. C. Byham, and J. M. Wilson. 1991. *Empowered Teams*. San Francisco: Jossey-Bass.

PERIODICALS AND JOURNALS

Automotive Engineering magazine
400 Commonwealth Dr. Warrendale, PA 15096-0001
(412) 776-4841

Barron's National Business & Financial Weekly
200 Liberty St.
New York, NY 10281-1003
(212) 416-2700

California Management Review
350 Barrows Hall
University of California–Berkeley
Berkeley, CA 94720
(510) 642-7159

The Canadian Manager
2175 Sheppard Ave. E, Suite 110
Willowdale, Ontario, M2J lW8 Canada
(416)) 493-0155

IEEE Engineering Management Review
345 East 47th St.
New York, NY 10017-2394
(212) 705-7366

Industrial Management
25 Technology Park/Atlanta
Norcross, GA 30092
(404) 449-0461

Journal of Systems Management
P.O. Box 38370
Cleveland, Ohio 44138-0370
(216) 243-6900

The Journal for Quality and Participation
801-B W. 8th St., #501
Cincinnati, Ohio 45203
(513) 381-1959

Manage
2210 Arbor Blvd.
Dayton, Ohio 45439-1506
(513) 294-0421

Management Review
135 W. 50th St.
New York, NY 10020-1201
(212) 903-8393

Manager's Magazine
P.O. Box 208
Hartford, CT 06141-0208
(203) 677-0033

Managing Automation
5 Penn Plaza
New York, NY 10001-1810
(212) 695-0500

Project Management Journal
P.O. Box 189
Webster, NC 28788
(704) 293-9711

Quality
191 Gary Avenue S.
Carol Stream, IL 60188
(708) 665-1000

Quality European Organization for Quality
P.O. Box 5032, CH-3001
Bem, Switzerland
031-216166

Quality Assurance
1250 6th Ave.
San Diego, CA 92101
(619) 230-1840

Quality Digest
1425 Vista Way, Box 1503
Red Bluff, CA 96080
(916) 527-8875

Quality Engineering
270 Madison Ave.
New York, NY 10016
(212) 696-9000

Quality Progress
611 E. Wisconsin Ave.
Milwaukee, WI 53201-3005
(414) 272-8575

Sloan Management Review
292 Main Street, E38-120
Cambridge, MA 02139
(617) 253-7170

World Policy Journal
65 5th Ave.
New York, NY 10003
(212) 229-5811